Palgrave Socio-Legal Studies

Series Editor
Dave Cowan
School of Law
University of Bristol
Bristol, UK

The Palgrave Socio-Legal Studies series is a developing series of monographs and textbooks featuring cutting edge work which, in the best tradition of socio-legal studies, reach out to a wide international audience.

More information about this series at
http://www.palgrave.com/gp/series/14679

Anna Carline • Clare Gunby
Jamie Murray

Rape and the Criminal Trial

Reconceptualising the Courtroom as an Affective Assemblage

Anna Carline
University of Liverpool
Liverpool, UK

Clare Gunby
Institute for Applied Health Research
University of Birmingham
Birmingham, UK

Jamie Murray
Liverpool Hope University
Liverpool, UK

Palgrave Socio-Legal Studies
ISBN 978-3-030-38686-3 ISBN 978-3-030-38684-9 (eBook)
https://doi.org/10.1007/978-3-030-38684-9

Cover illustration: Manfred Glueck/Alamy Stock Photo

This Palgrave Pivot imprint is published by the registered company Springer Nature Switzerland AG.
The registered company address is: Gewerbestrasse 11, 6330 Cham, Switzerland

Acknowledgements

There are a number of people to thank in the development and production of this book. Firstly, to our research participants, who were incredibly generous with their time, always accommodating and endlessly eloquent in the articulation of their views. Thanks also to all of those who helped us to access our participant group, sharing contacts or agreeing to disseminate information about the research. Thank you to the British Academy/ Leverhulme who supported the work through a Small Research Grant in the 2013–2014 round (grant number: SG131987); to colleagues and friends within the Schools of Law and Criminology at the University of Leicester and the Department of Law at Liverpool Hope; and finally, to the team at Palgrave Macmillan, for their flexibility and willingness to accommodate (more than once) extensions to our deadline. We hope you enjoy reading the book.

Contents

CHAPTER 1

Introduction

Abstract The unique argument developed in this book is that the criminal courtroom, specifically in rape cases, needs to be reconceptualised as a complex system and an 'affective assemblage'. We argue, for the first time, that a move beyond representational theory and towards new materialism and affects, which emphasises the importance of the 'ontological intensive regime', enables a more informed and realistic understanding of courtroom dynamics and the practices of barristers. This, in turn, impacts upon the implementation and utilisation of well-meaning reform measures and policies. In this first chapter, we introduce the philosophical framework and key concepts, which synthesises the work of Deleuze, Deleuze and Guattari and complexity science and theory. Thereafter, we set out the empirical and theoretical methodologies and briefly explain the criminal justice, law and policy context as it relates to rape.

Keywords Reconceptualising the courtroom • New materialism and affect theory • Affective assemblage • Methodologies • Problem field and phase space • Criminal justice responses to rape

A. Carline et al., *Rape and the Criminal Trial*, Palgrave Socio-Legal Studies, https://doi.org/10.1007/978-3-030-38684-9_1

1.1 Reconceptualising the Courtroom

The aims of this book revolve around three key themes. First, it sets out a novel theoretical and methodological approach for understanding and responding to social and legal problematics. Second, it develops new insights into criminal justice responses to sexual violence—with a focus on rape trials. Third, it calls for an essential re-orientation of criminal justice, criminology and legal studies, in light of the arguments progressed. Indeed, the overall argument developed is that the criminal courtroom needs to be reconceptualised as a complex system and an 'affective assemblage'. This, we maintain, enables a more informed and realistic understanding of courtroom dynamics and the practice of barristers, which in turn, impacts upon the implementation of measures and policies which aim to improve the criminal justice response to rape cases. In developing this argument, we recognise that the courtroom is a dramaturgical problem space, but one that involves non-representational drama.

Why make this argument? The first is the widely accepted assessment of the failure of existing criminal justice responses to rape and sexual violence (Lees 1997; HMCPSI and HMIC 2002, 2007; Kelly et al. 2005; Stern 2010; Cook 2011; HMIC and HMCPSI 2012) and the continued existence of an 'implementation gap' (Kelly et al. 2005; Stern 2010; Brown 2011; Cook 2011; Westmarland 2011; Smith 2018), whereby well-meaning measures are either not utilised or produce unanticipated results (see e.g. Carline and Gunby 2017). More radical and progressive work is therefore undoubtedly required to advance the area and to improve the experience of victims. Second, this book was conceived in the light of empirical work focused on barristers' perceptions and practices in relation to criminal justice responses to rape (see Gunby et al. 2010; Carline and Gunby 2011, 2017, 2019; Gunby and Carline 2019; Carline et al. in press). What brought this project together was the realisation that advocates' views and approaches to the courtroom revealed a legal world—a courtroom assemblage—which was very different from the doctrinal/socio-legal and representational model of that world. The data revealed that barristers lived and worked in a primarily material, affective and non-representational legal world, where orthodox understandings of law played at very best, a marginal role.

Thus, with reference to the three key themes we develop in this book, we maintain that it is not possible to devise effective criminal justice responses to rape until a thorough reconceptualisation of the criminal courtroom, as a complex system and an affective assemblage, has taken place. This reconceptualisation, in line with the legal world presented in barristers' interviews, is of the criminal courtroom as a matter of pragmatics, deployment and marshalling of affects, sense-making and the production of emergent truths.

In developing our key themes, there are a number of ramifications, implications, supplementary arguments and theoretical concepts to set out here, prior to elaboration in later chapters. First, there exists what is known as an 'intensive ontological register' to the social field and this book emphasises the necessity of taking up a Deleuzian ontology. This involves understanding the criminal courtroom as having a double existence. Namely, it exists on two very different but adjacent and interacting levels: one which is actual and extensive (which is ontology as we conventionally understand it) and the other which is real but intensive, concepts we explain in detail in Chaps. 2 and 6. Second, we argue that barristers, and indeed many court protagonists, intuitively operate in this intensive ontological field and have a rich appreciation and experience of working this register of the courtroom. Third, to our knowledge, there has been no utilisation of an ambitious theoretical framework like this to understand the courtroom as an intensive ontological field, or of how legal actors might intuitively work within this field. Relatedly, there has been no empirical exploration to date of how barristers' self-reflections on their professional practice evidence an intuitive understanding and participation within the intensive courtroom. Fourth, we maintain that the approach adopted in this book will improve our understanding of practitioners' perspectives and practices on the implementation of measures introduced to improve criminal justice responses to rape and sexual violence. Finally, there are significant methodological implications stemming from the approach developed here. These pertain to the adoption of a theoretical methodology of problem space, problematics and phase space, for thinking and working with affective assemblages, as well as the utilisation of a discursive empirical methodology for conducting and analysing the barrister interviews. This chapter will briefly introduce these methodologies.

To review, the overall aim of the book is to reconceptualise the criminal courtroom as a complex system and an affective assemblage. In so doing, we focus in particular on the changes to the substantive law introduced by the *Sexual Offences Act 2003* (specifically, the consent definition, presumptions and reformed mens rea), the introduction of judicial directions on 'mistaken assumptions' and the implementation of 'special measures'—

provisions which aim to support and protect the complainant during the trial process. Our reconceptualisation drives the development of a reflexive set of pragmatic and speculative techniques for examining, participating and intervening in affective assemblages. These techniques are concerned with rendering the indiscernible discernible, composing affects, articulating intensive bodies, triggering intensive processes, composing intensive planes of composition and the generation of truths (concepts all explored in Chaps. 2, 5 and 6). In addition, our reconceptualisation recognises that a new approach to the production and adoption of law reforms and policy is necessary in order to respond to the implementation gap. Here, our work resonates with and contributes to a broader, non-criminal justice literature which has argued that complex systems theory has much to offer implementation science (see e.g. Braithwaite et al. 2018) and promotes the adoption of adaptive management techniques, which are increasingly used to manage ecosystems.

1.2 Engaging with the Book: Affective and Non-representational Approaches

In a bid to advance an accessible discussion and foster an incremental understanding of what is a challenging philosophical framework, the book adopts a novel structure. In this chapter, we situate and introduce the philosophical framework and key concepts, set out the empirical and theoretical methodologies and briefly explain the criminal justice, law and policy context as it relates to rape. Chapter 2 commences by engaging in a mapping of the theoretical framework. This mapping provides a succinct yet comprehensive bringing together of the overall philosophical concepts and arguments. Following on, Chap. 2 introduces the data analysis by exploring a key ‘attractor’—that of conviction rates. The main objective of Chap. 2 is to enable the reader to develop a sense and understanding of how the various concepts work together in order to enable the courtroom to be reconceptualised and explored as a complex system and an affective assemblage.

Chapters 3 and 4 comprise the main data analysis. The former concentrates upon the ‘semiotic regime’, which pertains to key legal codes (i.e. the relevant rape provisions of the *Sexual Offences Act 2003*) along with the ‘mistaken assumptions directions’ (Judicial College 2019), which sit outside of the 2003 Act. Chapter 4 focuses more upon the ‘material regime', which relates to the performances of bodies in the courtroom. As will become clear, however, it is not possible to entirely separate these regimes, with the theoretical framework and empirical analysis being fundamentally, intricately and inexorably intertwined. These chapters have a dual objective: to develop radical and novel insights into the courtroom response to rape, as well as aid in the understanding of the theoretical framework adopted. Chapters 5 and 6 extend the understanding of our approach by setting out a more detailed and philosophically advanced exploration of the theoretical framework. Chapter 5 focuses upon Deleuze's materialist philosophy of affect and sense, encompassing a discussion of incorporeals, the intensive ontological regime, the problem field and phase space and the plane of composition. Chapter 6 explores in detail complex systems theory and Deleuze and Guattari's conceptualisation of affective assemblages. While these chapters appear after the discussion of the data, their content inspired and informed the analysis (see below for further justification of this approach). The conclusion considers what the arguments set out in this book mean for various audiences. Through discussion of techniques of affect, we conceive the work of affective professionals, such as barristers, to be artistic, political and (potentially) ethical. In addition to this, and in the context of research, policy development and implementation, we explore the concept and processes of adaptive management, in order to inform implementation practices.

Given our underpinning philosophical commitment, the chapters in this book have different 'speeds and slownesses'. They will 'affect'—inform and transform—different readers in divergent and maybe unexpected ways. We do not attempt to write in a single author voice; to do so would be to problematically ignore the 'intensive' reality of collaborative writing and the nature of the work. Indeed, it is important to recognise that the book itself is an affective assemblage. It does not need to be read in a linear fashion, nor in its entirety. While we have made an attempt to structure the chapters to provide the space for an incremental growth of knowledge and understanding, it may be that those readers who already have some appreciation of the theory want to start with Chaps. 5 and 6 (or indeed 6 and then 5) and reflect upon how these insights may be useful for their own areas of research and expertise. As we are aiming to be inclusive and write with numerous audiences in mind, including criminal justice practitioners and policymakers as well as academics (both novice and experienced in the theory), it may be that some readers are only interested in our key data findings and what this framework means in practice. They may therefore not want to delve into the philosophical genesis of the work and choose to focus on Chaps. 2, 3 and 4, along with the conclusion (in any order). Overall, the book aims to allow for engagement on many different levels and in divergent and non-determined pathways. In so doing, we promote an affective and non-representational approach to reading.

1.3 New Materialism and Affect Theory

In reconceptualising the courtroom as an affective assemblage, the book engages new materialism and affect theory to establish a theoretical framework and advance a set of philosophical concepts. Here, we situate some of the key elements of this approach. Materialism has enjoyed a renewal and increased popularity of late (Bennett 2010; Coole and Frost 2010; Braidotti 2013; Grosz 2017). In contrast to classical materialism, new materialism is informed by approaches that understand matter as dynamic and active—as opposed to passive and formed—while form is viewed as essential and active. It breaks with a recent dominant trend in theory of a primacy of language, structure and discourse and with an exclusive concern with the actual, states of affairs, functions and conceptual frameworks of essences, universals, reductionism and representation. Intersecting with this new materialism is the 'affective turn', which focuses upon the body—both fleshy and otherwise—and embodied lived experiences. As Wetherell explains: 'The turn to affect … leads to a focus on embodiment, to attempts to understand how people are moved, and what attracts them, to an emphasis on repetitions, pains and pleasures, feelings and memories' (2012: 2). New materialism and affect theory are broadly characterised by a primacy of process, philosophy of immanence, of force, powers and affects and of how they compose form, of ontology as ontogenesis and the germinal life of an immanent relationality. They theorise a world of 'becoming' in place of a world of 'being'.

There are many different strands to new materialism and the 'affective turn' in contemporary theory (Clough and Halley 2007; Bennett 2010; Coole and Frost 2010; Gregg and Seigworth 2010; Wetherell 2012; Dolphijn and Van der Tuin 2012; Massumi 2015; Grosz 2017). Such approaches have been particularly utilised in the humanities and social sciences; though to date, there has been limited application in criminology, criminal justice and legal studies (notable exceptions include Milovanovic 2018; Philippopoulos-Mihalopoulos 2015). In this book, the broad theoretical framework of new materialism and the affective turn is taken up as a synthesis of Deleuze and Guattari's affective assemblage theory, underpinned by Deleuze's materialist philosophy of affect and sense and complexity science and theory. This finds its theoretical provenance in the work of Deleuze and Guattari's social assemblage theory (2017, 1986, 2004, 1994),[1] Deleuze on affect and sense (1990, 1991, 1992), complexity science and theory (Waldrop 1992; Kauffman 1995, 2000; Coveney and Highfield 1995), supplemented by the various broader sources from affect theory and assemblage theory (Massumi 1992, 2002; Delanda 2000, 2006; Braidotti 2013; Grosz 2017).

Our synthetic paradigm involves an explicit shift beyond representational models. We move towards frameworks that focus upon the existence of the intensive ontological register, which sits alongside—or is adjacent to and doubles—the ontology of an extensive actual register, with complex processes of relay occurring between the two. This intensive register is populated by incorporeal matter, bodies and forces, affect-events, attractors and singularities and processes of self-organisation and emergence. This novel theoretical framework and set of concepts includes a new understanding of sense-making, the production of truth and the drawing of two planes—one of extensive organisation and the other of intensive composition. As noted, at its centre is Deleuze and Guattari's affective assemblage theory, with assemblages comprising a semiotic and a material regime, which are in interconnection and interaction and experience profound processes of territorialisation, deterritorialisation and reterritorialisation. In our synthesis, the methodology of problem space, the problematic and phase space are vital, as are the concepts of mapping complex assemblages in high dimensionality manifolds and distributions of singularities. We explore all these concepts in Chaps. 2, 5 and 6.

1.4 Empirical and Theoretical Methodologies

There are two key methodological issues specific to this book. The first relates to the empirical methodology of collating and analysing barristers' viewpoints on the affective nature and dynamics of the courtroom in rape cases. The second pertains to the exploration of the incorporeal intensive field of the courtroom, which entails the adoption of a theoretical framework that is non-representational. This non-representational methodology is the idea of problem space, problematics and phase space.[2]

1.4.1 Methodology One: Exploring Affects Through Interviews with Barristers

Supported by British Academy funding, between 2015 and 2016 two of the authors (Carline and Gunby) conducted 39 semi-structured interviews with barristers who prosecuted and defended in English rape cases (see Gunby and Carline 2019 for further details of our methodology). In order to attain a purposive sample, participants were recruited from the four largest cities in the four Crown Prosecution Service (CPS) regions that prosecuted the most rapes in 2011–2012 (CPS 2012). We interviewed 6 barristers from two chambers in the largest city in the West Midlands; 6 barristers from two chambers in the largest city in Yorkshire and Humberside; 9 barristers from three chambers in the largest city in the North West; and 18 barristers from nine chambers in London. We sampled from roughly one-quarter of chambers that specialised in crime in each city.

Barristers were recruited via a range of methods. These included snowballing of existing contacts, emailing practitioners identified from their chamber's websites as having experience in rape cases and liaising with the clerks of chambers that dealt heavily with sex crimes to ask them to disseminate information about the research. The final sample consisted of 18 men and 21 women, the majority of which were highly experienced. Experience ranged from four years working on rape cases, through to in excess of 40. At the time of interview, over half of the sample said that at least 50% of their workload involved rape. Thirty-four participants had a mixed practice of defending and prosecuting, whilst four only defended and one exclusively prosecuted sex offences. Barristers had experience working on a range of historic and contemporary sexual violence cases, including stranger, acquaintance, adult and child rape, where women, girls, men and boys were the complainant. However, due to the gendered nature of rape (ONS 2018), females were most frequently situated as the victim and their cases discussed accordingly. As such, and following the language of barristers, we use female pronouns when referring to victims/survivors/complainants, unless the advocate explicitly stated otherwise.

Interviews took place in chambers, at court or over the telephone (14 interviews were telephone interviews) and lasted an average of 57 minutes. The semi-structured interview schedule was devised following review of our previous study data (Gunby et al. 2010; Carline and Gunby 2011, 2017) and relevant literature. Questions teased out participants' views on the implementation of the *Sexual Offences Act 2003*, the impact of policy developments, judicial directions and the use of special measures, in addition to issues relating to rates of conviction and attrition. Interviews were digitally recorded and transcribed immediately after they had been conducted. This enabled the identification of additional lines of inquiry which were pursued in subsequent interviews. Transcripts were independently scrutinised and coded to identify broad concepts and categories, using NVivo qualitative analysis software. Following the development of a set of coded themes transcripts were re-read, discussed and agreed by the authors to ensure consistency in their allocation, structuring and to refine concepts and theory.

Barristers are a relatively under-researched group and we argue here, as we have elsewhere, that it is vital to continually engage with practitioners to develop a grounded appreciation of how measures work (or otherwise) in practice. Engaging with those who are part of the courtroom affective assemblage is necessary to gathering data on, and understanding, the dynamics and processes of that complex system. Hence, it is pivotal to our new materialist synthetic paradigm.

1.4.2 Methodology Two: Problem Space, Problematics and Phase Space

As we have noted, our new materialist and affective theoretical framework breaks with the orthodox reductionist and representational paradigms. Instead, there is the adoption of a framework underpinned by philosophical commitment to an intensive ontological register that doubles the extensive actual register. Exploration of this register and the complex systems that participate in it are characterised by interconnectivity of process, openness of systems, dynamic boundaries, self-organisation and emergence and intensive processes of composition: factors not well captured within reductionist paradigm and representational frameworks. As Deleuze commented as early as *Difference and Repetition*, ‘systems of simulacra [intensive ontological complexity] must be described with the help of notions which, from the outset, are very different from the categories of representation’ (1994: 363). Underpinning the creativity and novelty of new materialist philosophy and complexity theory is a mathematical methodology of phase space and an understanding of intensive problem space. Phase space is a way to conceptualise the dynamics of complex processes and systems. It involves mathematical tools of differential calculus, vector fields, degrees of freedom, high dimensionality manifolds, distributions of singularities, non-Euclidean topologies, multiplicities and phase space portraits. Significantly, there is direct association between the concept of problem space and the understanding of the intensive ontological register. Understanding the dynamics of an affective assemblage (i.e. the courtroom) involves understanding, and mapping, the problem space of that assemblage. It is this methodology that underlies the Deleuzian new materialist and affect theory theoretical framework. It is this same framework that informs our synthesis of Deleuze and Guattari's affective assemblage theory, Deleuze's materialist philosophy of affect and sense and complexity theory. As noted, the theoretical framework adopted here is very different to a reductionist and representational framework and is radically novel and transdisciplinary. It opens up a previously indiscernible and imperceptible intensive world and offers new ways of thinking about this world.

Thus, in combining the two methodologies, we read the barrister data in order to gain an understanding of, and map out in phase space, the affects and intensive relationships between different actors and elements of the courtroom affective assemblage. We explore the attractors and singularities, affect-events, lines of flights and processes of territorialisation, deterritorialisation and reterritorialisation. Adopting this approach renders perceptible the intensive ontological regime and the problem space of the courtroom in rape cases, so as to produce a new sense and truth of that courtroom. This enables an understanding of what drives barristers' practice, which sheds light on factors pertaining to the implementation and impact of law reforms and policy measures. This understanding, we argue, is pivotal to appreciating whether (and why) reform measures will be adopted in the courtroom setting and thus is vital knowledge for practitioners, legislatures and policymakers, as well as those researching sexual violence.

1.5 Setting the Scene: Criminal Justice Responses to Rape

In this final section, we provide an overview of certain measures pertaining to the criminal justice response to rape, which underpin the basis of our data analysis. There is a voluminous literature which explores the shortcomings of the system's response to rape/sexual violence, with successive governments in England and Wales (as elsewhere) introducing a plenitude of reforms, reviews and policy documents, aiming to improve that response (see Home Office 2000, 2002, 2006; CPS and Police 2002, 2015; Stern 2010). However, despite substantial reform, 'little really changes' (Cook 2011: 257. See also Jordan 2001; Brown 2011), with research highlighting the problem of an 'implementation gap', or more specifically, the failure of certain policies to filter down into practice (see e.g. Lees 1997; Kelly et al. 2005; Stern 2010; Cook, 2011; Carline and Gunby 2017; Smith 2018). As is well known, concerns exist around high attrition and low conviction rates. While there has been a dramatic increase in the number of police reported rapes in England and Wales since the 1940s (Gregory and Lees 1996; Temkin and Krahe 2008; Hohl and Stanko 2015), the vast majority, around 89%, remain unreported (MoJ et al. 2013). Of those cases that are reported, the rate of conviction continues to be around 6% (MoJ et al. 2013), a substantial decrease from 32% in 1979 (Temkin and Krahe 2008).

A wealth of literature also explores the problematic treatment of rape victims within the criminal justice system and the extent, and impact, of secondary victimisation (see e.g. Lees 1997; Temkin and Krahe 2008; Payne 2009; Stern 2010; Smith 2018). Feminist scholars have long highlighted a 'culture of scepticism' that has impacted justice responses (Kelly et al. 2005: 83). Concerns exist around the ongoing circulation and impact of rape myths and misconceptions on all actors within the system (see e.g. Temkin and Krahe 2008; Ellison and Munro 2009, 2010a; Smith and Skinner 2017; Smith 2018). These include notions of stranger rape as 'real rape', that a 'real victim' would resist, suffer physical injuries and report the crime immediately, that false allegations are common and victims who drink exacerbate their victimisation (see e.g. Lonsway and Fitzgerald 1994; Saunders 2012; Smith 2018). These discourses influence key decision-making processes at all points of the justice process (Kelly et al. 2005; Temkin and Krahe 2008; Finch and Munro 2005, 2007; Ellison and Munro 2009, 2010a, 2010b; Carline and Easteal 2014; Hohl and Stanko 2015), from a victim's initial decision to report, police and prosecutorial decisions to arrest, charge and prosecute, through to the juries' ultimate verdict.

1.5.1 Substantive Law: Sexual Offences Act 2003

The legal landscape of sex crimes underwent significant reform in 2003, with the then labour government having high hopes for the resulting product—the *Sexual Offences Act 2003*. The reform and political context is well known and we do not wish to repeat that here. Suffice it to state that the Act was developed in the context of increasing rates of attrition and decreasing rates of conviction with it being hoped that, in addition to modernising the law, the new provisions would remedy these problems (see Home Office 2000, 2002, 2006; Temkin and Ashworth 2004; Gunby et al. 2010; Carline and Easteal 2014). The offence of rape as set out in s.1 states:

1. A person (A) commits an offence if—
   (a) he intentionally penetrates the vagina, anus or mouth of another person (B) with his penis,
   (b) B does not consent to the penetration, and
   (c) A does not reasonably believe that B consents.
2. Whether a belief is reasonable is to be determined having regard to all the circumstances, including any steps A has taken to ascertain whether B consents.

The Statutory Definition of Consent

Research has amply demonstrated that the increase in allegations of acquaintance and relationship rape (as opposed to strange rape) has culminated in a decreasing conviction rate (Lees 1997; Kelly et al. 2005; Hohl and Stanko 2015). In a bid to assist the jury on determining the issue of consent and introducing greater legal clarity, New Labour introduced for the first time a statutory consent definition that states: 'A person consents if he agrees by choice, and has the freedom and capacity to make that choice' (s.74). It was surmised that the definition was 'clear and unambiguous' and a significant improvement on the prior common law (Home Office 2002: 16). The adequacy (or otherwise) of this definition has been well debated (see e.g. Temkin and Ashworth 2004; Finch and Munro 2006; Tadros 2006; Cowan 2007; Elliot and de Than 2007; Gunby et al. 2010), and we do not wish to repeat those debates here.

Mens Rea: Reasonable Belief in Consent

During the reform process, concerns also focused on the previous subjective test, set down in *DPP v Morgan* ([1976]), 'contribute[ing] in some part to the low rate of convictions for rape' (Home Office 2002: 17). This was due to the assumption that an honest yet unreasonable belief in consent could enable a defendant to avoid a rape conviction. Under the

Sexual Offences Act 2003 s.1(3), any belief in consent must now be reasonable and the law places a level of responsibility onto the defendant to ensure that the complainant was consenting. Indeed, the jury is entitled to take into account 'any steps A has taken to ascertain whether B consents' (s.1(2)). However, the reform has been critiqued on the basis that when taking into account 'all the circumstances', so as to determine whether the belief was reasonable, this may permit a jury to consider stereotypical and sexist views regarding appropriate female behaviour (Temkin and Ashworth 2004). Furthermore, it may enable jurors to place undue emphasis upon the complainant's activity in the timeframe prior to the sexual encounter and draw problematic inferences from behaviour such as flirting or inviting a person back for coffee (Ellison and Munro 2009).

Evidential and Conclusive Presumptions

A further critical addition to the 2003 Act was the introduction of s.75 and s.76, where, upon the production of sufficient evidence by the prosecution, the law will presume that (a) the complainant did not consent and (b) the defendant did not hold a reasonable belief in consent. While those presumptions contained in s.75 may be rebutted by the defendant upon the production of adequate evidence, the s.76 presumptions are conclusive in nature. Consequently, s.75 covers a wider range of circumstances and acts including the use of violence and/or the threat of violence (either to the complainant or a third party) and cases in which the complainant is asleep, unconscious, unlawfully detained, unable to express consent due a disability or involuntarily intoxicated. During the reform process, it was anticipated that the presumptions would assist the jury with the 'fundamental question' of whether the complainant did consent to the sexual intercourse and 'send a clear signal to the public about the circumstances in which sexual activity is likely to be wrong' (Home Office 2002: 16).

Under s.75, a judge will determine whether a presumption arises and whether the defendant has raised sufficient evidence to rebut it (Home Office 2002; *R v Zhang* [2007]). Commentators surmised that little evidence would be necessary in order for a defendant to convince the judge that the presumption had been rebutted (Finch and Munro 2004) and our previous research supports this contention (Gunby et al. 2010; Carline and Gunby 2011). At the same time, the Court of Appeal in *R v Ciccarelli* made it clear that evidence beyond 'fanciful or speculative' is required to discharge the burden ([2011] 18). Section 76 is limited to cases in which the defendant intentionally deceives the complainant to either his identity or the nature and purpose of the act. The restricted definition of 'nature and purpose' was confirmed by the Court of Appeal in *R v Jheeta* [2007], in which the court held that a deception was limited to misconceptions regarding the physical act that was taking place, as opposed to the use of 'common garden lies' to persuade the complainant to agree to engage in sexual intercourse (see further Gunby et al. 2010; Carline and Gunby 2011; Carline and Easteal 2014).

1.5.2 Mistaken Assumptions Directions

A more recent innovation has been the introduction of directions pertaining to 'mistaken assumptions' in rape and sexual violence cases, delivered by the judge to the jury during summing up. Developed by the judicial college and initially introduced in 2010, these directions aim to tackle various stereotypes 'which could lead the jury to approach the complainant's evidence with unwarranted scepticism' (Judicial Studies Board 2010: 356; Judicial College 2019). They represent a progressive move as they address many of the concerns highlighted in academic literature around the impact of myths on rape cases. Given the extent to which research suggests juries' decisions are overwhelmingly informed by (problematic) scripts, as opposed to the law (Kelly et al. 2005; Finch and Munro 2005, 2007; Temkin and Krahe 2008; Ellison and Munro 2009, 2010a, 2010b; Smith and Skinner 2017), they are arguably more important than the relevant legal provisions. These directions relate, but are not limited to delays in reporting, the failure to physically or verbally resist, a lack of physical injury, the victim's attire, demeanour and intoxication. They also cover the existence of a previous relationship and/or sexual activity between the defendant and the complainant, inconsistencies in the victim's testimony and the emotions/distress (or lack thereof) displayed by the complainant at trial (for a discussion see Temkin 2010; Smith and Skinner 2017; Temkin et al. 2018).

1.5.3 Special Measures

Introduced by the *Youth Justice and Criminal Evidence Act 1999* (*YJCEA*), special measures aim to enable and support those witnesses who are vulnerable or intimidated (VIWs) to participate more effectively within the criminal justice system (Home Office 1998). Recognising that many VIWs may be reluctant to come forward and report allegations and/or provide testimony, special measures aim to offer reassurance and protection, ameliorate the stress and anxiety of giving evidence during a trial and to ultimately improve the quality of the testimony elicited (Home Office 1998). These measures comprise screens to shield the witness from the accused (s.23), giving evidence via a live link (s.24) or in private (s.25), removal of wigs and gowns (s.26), video recorded evidence in chief (s.27), video recorded cross-examination and re-examination (s.28) and examination through intermediary (s.29). Early evaluation indicated that VIWs were enabled, assisted and supported by special measures, with 33% indicating that they would not have been willing to testify without them (Hamlyn et al. 2004: 78; see also Burton et al. 2006). Under s.17, a sexual violence complainant is considered an intimidated witness on the basis that they are likely to suffer fear and apprehension when giving their evidence. They may also be considered 'vulnerable', meaning that they require assistance due to age and/or incapacity (s.16).

In addition to these statutory provisions, guidance is provided by the Ministry of Justice in the form of Achieving Best Evidence in Criminal Justice Proceedings (MoJ 2011). Of particular import, police are recommended to use the 'cognitive interview' technique when conducting the investigatory interview with the complainant, as it has been shown to increase the accuracy and completeness of the evidence provided (Köhnken et al. 1999; Memon et al. 2010). This interview should be video recorded and may be played in court as the complainant's evidence in chief (referred to as the ABE interview). As set out in the guidance, the cognitive interview comprises a four-phased approach: (1) rapport building, (2) free narrative account, (3) questioning and (4) closing the interview. During the second phase, the complainant should be able to provide an uninterrupted free narrative account of the incident, with the interviewer engaging in 'active listening' and, when necessary, using 'non-specific prompts' to elicit further information (MoJ 2011: 74). The interviewer may ask specific questions in phase three, based upon the information garnered during the prior phase. This should allow the complainant to produce a more detailed recollection, supported by the admonishment of the use of closed and leading questions.

The use of technology may do little to neutralise the ordeal of being cross-examined (Hamlyn et al. 2004) and it remains to be seen whether the implementation of pre-recorded cross-examination ameliorates some of the distress caused by this process (MoJ and HMCTS 2016). In addition, the Court of Appeal has recently issued guidance which aims to curtail the worst excesses of cross-examination techniques in cases involving intimidated (although not vulnerable) witnesses, particularly children. In *R v Barker*, the Court stated that advocates were to 'adapt … cross-examination … to enable the child to give the best evidence of which he or she is capable' ([2010] 42. See also *R v W & M* [2010]; *R v Edwards* [2011]; *R v Wills* [2011]; *R v Farooqi* [2013]). Correspondingly, the Advocate's Gateway (2019) sets out that examination techniques and questions should be discussed pre-trial with the judge and an intermediary (if one is involved) in a ground rules hearing. This is to ensure that questions are appropriately adapted to enable the vulnerable witness to participate in, and communicate effectively during, the trial (for a detailed analysis of these developments see e.g. Keane 2012; Plotnikoff and Woolfson 2012; Henderson 2014, 2016).

1.6 Conclusion

In reconceptualising the courtroom as an affective assemblage, the book involves a decisive move away from a representational framework. Moreover, it is the first to set out a new materialist synthetic paradigm that draws together theories of affect, complexity and assemblage theory and to set forth the intensive ontological register as fundamental to this account. This leads us to explicate a novel theoretical and methodological approach for understanding and responding to social and legal problematics. While our project focuses upon rape cases, the theoretical and methodological approach undoubtedly has a wider resonance and we encourage its application to other areas of criminal justice, criminology and legal studies.

Notes

1. The references are listed in order of the *original* publication date, as opposed to the publication date of the edition referenced. This is to enable the reader to develop an understanding of the trajectory of the work.
2. On Deleuzian-inspired methodologies and researching affects, see also Coleman and Ringrose (2013) and Knudsen and Stage (2015).

References

Advocate's Gateway. (2019). Ground Rules Hearings and the Fair Treatment of Vulnerable People in Court. *The Advocate's Gateway*. Retrieved September 6, 2019, from https://www.theadvocatesgateway.org/images/toolkits/1-ground-rules-hearings-and-the-fair-treatment-of-vulnerable-people-in-court-2019.pdf.

Bennett, J. (2010). *Vibrant Matter: A Political Ecology of Things*. Durham: Duke University Press.

Braidotti, R. (2013). *The Posthuman*. Cambridge: Polity Press.

Braithwaite, J., Churrca, K., Long, J. C., Ellis, L. A., & Herkes, J. (2018). When Complexity Science Meets Implementation Science: A Theoretical Empirical Analysis of Systems Change. *BMC Medicine, 16*(63), 1–14.

Brown, J. (2011). We Mind and We Care but Have Things Changed? Assessment of Progress in the Reporting, Investigating and Prosecution of Allegations of Rape. *Journal of Sexual Aggression, 17*(1), 1–10.

Burton, M., Evans, R., & Sanders, A. (2006). *Are Special Measures for Vulnerable and Intimidated Witnesses Working? Evidence from the Criminal Justice Agencies*. London: Home Office.

Carline, A., & Easteal, P. (2014). *Shades of Grey – Domestic and Sexual Violence Against Women: Law Reform and Society*. Abingdon: Routledge.

Carline, A., & Gunby, G. (2011). 'How an Ordinary Jury Makes Sense of It Is a Mystery': Barristers' Perspectives on Rape, Consent and the Sexual Offences Act 2003. *Liverpool Law Review, 32*(3), 237–250.

Carline, A., & Gunby, C. (2017). Rape Politics, Policies and Practice: Exploring the Tensions and Unanticipated Consequences of Well-Intended Victim-Focused Measures. *The Howard Journal of Crime and Justice, 56*(1), 34–52.

Carline, A., & Gunby, C. (2019). Justice for Rape Complainants: Limitations and Possibilities. In P. Carlen & L. A. Franca (Eds.), *Justice Alternatives* (pp. 306–320). Abingdon: Routledge.

Carline, A., Gunby, C., & Murray, J. (in press). "And That's Why Street-Wise Complainants Now Always Give Evidence Behind Screens, Live": Exploring the Intensive Affects of the Courtroom. In K. Duncanson & E. Henderson (Eds.), *Courthouse Design and Social Justice*. Routledge.

Clough, P., & Halley, J. (Eds.). (2007). *The Affective Turn: Theorising the Social*. Durham: Duke University Press.

Coleman, R., & Ringrose, J. (Eds.). (2013). *Deleuze and Research Methodologies*. Edinburgh: Edinburgh University Press.

Cook, K. (2011). Rape Investigation and Prosecution: Stuck in the Mud? *Journal of Sexual Aggression, 17*, 250–262.

Coole, D., & Frost, S. (2010). *New Materialism: Ontology, Agency and Politics*. Durham: Duke University Press.

Coveney, P., & Highfield, R. (1995). *Frontiers of Complexity: The Search for Order in a Chaotic World.* London: Faber and Faber.

Cowan, S. (2007). 'Freedom and Capacity to Make a Choice': A Feminist Analysis of Consent in the Criminal Law of Rape. In V. E. Munro & C. F. Stychin (Eds.), *Sexuality and the Law: Feminist Engagements* (pp. 51–72). Abingdon: Routledge-Cavendish.

Crown Prosecution Service (CPS). (2012). *Violence Against Women and Girls Crime Report 2011–2012.* London: CPS.

Crown Prosecution Service (CPS) and Police. (2002). *Joint CPS and Police Action Plan on Rape.* London: CPS.

Crown Prosecution Service (CPS) and Police. (2015). *Joint CPS and Police Action Plan on Rape.* London: CPS.

Delanda, M. (2000). *A Thousand Years of Nonlinear History.* New York: Zone Books.

Delanda, M. (2006). *A New Philosophy of Society: Assemblage Theory and Social Complexity.* London: Continuum.

Deleuze, G. (1990). *Logic of Sense.* London: Athlone Press.

Deleuze, G. (1991). *Bergsonism.* New York: Zone Books.

Deleuze, G. (1992). *Expressionism in Philosophy: Spinoza.* New York: Zone Books.

Deleuze, G. (1994). *Difference and Repetition.* London: Athlone Press.

Deleuze, G., & Guattari, F. (1986). *Kafka: Toward a Minor Literature.* Minneapolis: University of Minnesota Press.

Deleuze, G., & Guattari, F. (1994). *What Is Philosophy?* London: Verso.

Deleuze, G., & Guattari, F. (2004). *A Thousand Plateaus.* London: Continuum.

Deleuze, G., & Guattari, F. (2017). *Anti-Oedipus.* London: Bloomsbury.

Dolphijn, R., & Van der Tuin, I. (2012). *New Materialism: Interviews and Cartographies.* Michigan: Open Humanities Press.

Elliott, C., & de Than, C. (2007). The Case for a Rational Reconstruction of Consent in Criminal Law. *Modern Law Review, 70*(2), 225–249.

Ellison, L., & Munro, V. E. (2009). Reacting to Rape: Exploring Mock Jurors' Assessments of Complainant Credibility. *British Journal of Criminology, 49*(2), 202–219.

Ellison, L., & Munro, V. E. (2010a). Getting to (Not) Guilty: Examining Jurors' Deliberative Processes in and Beyond the Context of a Mock Rape Trial. *Legal Studies, 30*(1), 74–97.

Ellison, L., & Munro, V. E. (2010b). A Stranger in the Bushes, or an Elephant in the Room? Critical Reflection upon Received Rape Myth Wisdom in the Context of a Mock Jury Study. *New Criminal Law Review, 13*(4), 781–801.

Finch, E., & Munro, V. E. (2004). The Sexual Offences Act 2003: Intoxicated Consent and Drug Assisted Rape Revisited. *Criminal Law Review, October*, 789–802.

Finch, E., & Munro, V. E. (2005). Juror Stereotypes and Blame Attribution in Rape Cases Involving Intoxicants: The Finding of a Pilot Study. *British Journal of Criminology, 45*(1), 25–38.

Finch, E., & Munro, V. (2006). Breaking Boundaries? Sexual Consent in the Jury Room. *Legal Studies, 26*(3), 303–320.

Finch, E., & Munro, V. E. (2007). The Demon Drink and the Demonised Woman: Socio-Sexual Stereotypes and Responsibility Attribution in Rape Trials Involving Intoxicants. *Social and Legal Studies, 16*(4), 591–614.

Gregory, S., & Lees, J. (1996). Attrition in Rape and Sexual Assault Cases. *The British Journal of Criminology, 36*(1), 1–36.

Gregg, M., & Seigworth, E. (2010). *The Affect Theory Reader*. Durham: Duke University Press.

Grosz, E. (2017). *The Incorporeal: Ontology, Ethics, and the Limits of Materialism*. New York: Columbia University Press.

Gunby, C., & Carline, A. (2019). The Emotional Particulars of Working on Rape Cases: Doing Dirty Work, Managing Emotional Dirt and Conceptualizing 'Tempered Indifference'. *British Journal of Criminology*. https://doi.org/10.1093/bjc/azz054.

Gunby, C., Carline, A., & Beynon, C. (2010). Alcohol Related Rape Cases: Barristers' Perspectives on the Sexual Offences Act 2003 and Its Impact on Practice. *Journal of Criminal Law, 74*(6), 579–600.

Hamlyn, B., Phelps, A., Turtle, J., & Sattar, G. (2004). *Are Special Measures Working? Evidence from Surveys of Vulnerable and Intimidated Witnesses*. London: Home Office.

Henderson, E. (2014). All the Proper Protections – the Court of Appeal Rewrites the Rules from the Cross-Examination of Vulnerable Witnesses. *Criminal Law Review, 2*, 93–108.

Henderson, E. (2016). Taking Control of Cross-Examination: Judges, Advocates and Intermediaries Discuss Judicial Management of the Cross-Examination of Vulnerable People. *Criminal Law Review, 3*, 181–205.

HM Crown Prosecution Service Inspectorate (HMCPSI) and HM Inspectorate of Constabulary (HMIC). (2002). *A Report on the Joint Inspection into the Investigation and Prosecution of Cases Involving Allegations of Rape*. London: HMIC.

HM Crown Prosecution Service Inspectorate (HMCPSI) and HM Inspectorate of Constabulary (HMIC). (2007). *Without Consent: A Report on the Joint Review of the Investigation and Prosecution of Rape Offences*. London: HMIC.

HM Inspectorate of Constabulary (HMIC) and HM Crown Prosecution Service Inspectorate (HMCPSI). (2012). *Forging the Links: Rape Investigation and Prosecutions: A Joint Review by HMIC and HMCPSI*. London: HMIC.

Hohl, K., & Stanko, B. (2015). Complaints of Rape and the Criminal Justice System: Fresh Evidence on the Attrition Problem in England and Wales. *European Journal of Criminology, 12*(3), 324–341.

Home Office. (1998). *Speaking up for Justice: Report of the Interdepartmental Working Group on the Treatment of Vulnerable or Intimidated Witnesses in the Criminal Justice System*. London: Home Office.

Home Office. (2000). *Setting the Boundaries: Reforming the Law on Sex Offences* (Vol. 1). London: Home Office.

Home Office. (2002). *Protecting the Public: Strengthening Protection Against Sex Offenders and Reforming the Law of Sexual Offences*. London: Home Office.

Home Office. (2006). *Convicting Rapists and Protecting Victims – Justice for Victims of Rape*. London: Home Office.

Jordan, J. (2001). Worlds Apart? Women, Rape and the Reporting Process. *British Journal of Criminology, 41*, 679–706.

Judicial College. (2019). *The Crown Court Compendium. Part 1: Trial Management and Summing Up*. London: Judicial College.

Judicial Studies Board. (2010). *Crown Court Bench Book: Directing the Jury*. London: Judicial Studies Board.

Kauffman, S. (1995). *At Home in the Universe: The Search for Laws of Self-Organisation and Complexity*. Oxford: Oxford University Press.

Kauffman, S. (2000). *Investigations*. Oxford: Oxford University Press.

Keane, A. (2012). Towards a Principled Approach to the Cross-Examination of Vulnerable Witnesses. *Criminal Law Review, 6*, 407–420.

Kelly, L., Lovett, J., & Regan, L. (2005). *A Gap or a Chasm? Attrition in Reported Rape Cases*. Home Office Research Study 293, Home Office Research, Development and Statistics Directorate. London: Home Office.

Knudsen, B. T., & Stage, C. (Eds.). (2015). *Affective Methodologies: Developing Cultural Research for the Study of Affect*. Basingstoke: Palgrave Macmillan.

Köhnken, G., Milne, R., Memon, A., & Bull, R. (1999). The Cognitive Interview: A Meta-Analysis. *Psychology, Crime and Law, 5*(1–2), 3–27.

Lees, S. (1997). *Carnal Knowledge: Rape on Trial*. Harmondsworth: Penguin Books.

Lonsway, K., & Fitzgerald, L. (1994). Rape Myths: In Review. *Psychology of Women Quarterly, 18*(2), 133–164.

Massumi, B. (1992). *A User's Guide to Capitalism and Schizophrenia: Deviations from Deleuze and Guattari*. Massachusetts: MIT Press.

Massumi, B. (2002). *Parables for the Virtual: Movement, Affect, Sensation*. Durham: Duke University Press.

Massumi, B. (2015). *Politics of Affect*. Cambridge: Polity Press

Memon, A., Meissner, C. A., & Fraser, J. (2010). The Cognitive Interview: A Meta-Analytic Review and Study Space Analysis of the Past 25 Years. *Psychology, Public Policy, and Law, 16*(4), 340–372.

Milovanovic, D. (2018). Diversity, Law and Justice: A Deleuzian semiotic view of 'criminal justice'. *International Journal of the Semiotic of Law, 20*, 55–79.

Ministry of Justice (MoJ). (2011). *Achieving Best Evidence in Criminal Proceedings Guidance on Interviewing Victims and Witnesses, and Guidance on Using Special Measures*. London: Ministry of Justice.

Ministry of Justice (MoJ) and HM Courts and Tribunal Service (HMCTS). (2016). *Process Evaluation of Pre-Recorded Cross-Examination Pilot (Section 28)*. London: Ministry of Justice.

Ministry of Justice (MoJ), Home Office, and Office for National Statistics (ONS). (2013). *An Overview of Sexual Offending in England and Wales*. London: Ministry of Justice, Home Office, and ONS.

Office for National Statistics (ONS). (2018). *Sexual Offences in England and Wales: Year Ending March 2017*. London: Office for National Statistics.

Payne, S. (2009). *Redefining Justice: Addressing the Individual Needs of Victims and Witnesses*. London: Home Office.

Philippopoulos-Mihalopoulos, A. (2015). *Spatial Justice: Body, Lawscape, Atmosphere*. Abingdon: Routledge.

Plotnikoff, J., & Woolfson, R. (2012). Kicking and Screaming: The Slow Road to Best Evidence. In J. R. Spencer & M. Lamb (Eds.), *Children and Cross-Examination: Time to Change the Rules?* (pp. 21–42). Oxford: Hart.

Saunders, A. (2012). *Speech on the Prosecution of Rape and Serious Sexual Offences by Alison Saunders, Chief Crown Prosecutor for London*. London: CPS.

Smith, O. (2018). *Rape Trials in England and Wales: Observing Justice and Rethinking Rape Myths*. London: Palgrave Macmillan.

Smith, O., & Skinner, T. (2017). How Rape Myths Are Used and Challenged in Rape and Sexual Assault Trials. *Social and Legal Studies, 26*(4), 441–466.

Stern Review. (2010). *A Report by Baroness Vivien Stern CBE of an Independent Review into How Rape Complaints Are Handled by Public Authorities in England and Wales*. London: Home Office.

Tadros, V. (2006). Rape Without Consent. *Oxford Journal of Legal Studies, 26*(3), 515–543.

Temkin, J. (2010). "And Always Keep A-Hold of Nurse, for Fear of Finding Something Worse": Challenging Rape Myths in the Courtroom. *New Criminal Law Review, 13*(4), 710–734.

Temkin, J., & Ashworth, A. (2004). The Sexual Offences Act 2003: (1) Rape, Sexual Assaults and the Problems of Consent. *Criminal Law Review, May*, 328–346.

Temkin, J., & Krahe, B. (2008). *Sexual Assault and the Justice Gap: A Question of Attitude*. Oxford: Hart Publishing.

Temkin, J., Gray, J. M., & Barrett, J. (2018). Different Function of Rape Myth Use in Court: Findings from a Trial Observation Study. *Feminist Criminology, 13*(2), 205–225.

Waldrop, M. (1992). *Complexity: The Emerging Science at the Edge of Order and Chaos*. Simon and Schuster.

Westmarland, N. (2011). Still Little Justice for Rape Victim Survivors: The Void Between Policy and Practice in England and Wales. In N. Westmarland & G. Gangoli (Eds.), *International Approaches to Rape* (pp. 79–100). Bristol: Policy Press.

Wetherell, M. (2012). *Affect and Emotion: A New Social Science Understanding*. London: Sage.

Case List

R v Barker [2010] EWCA Crim 4.
R v Ciccarelli [2011] EWCA 2665.
R v Edwards [2011] EWCA Crim 3028.
R v Farooqi [2013] EWCA Crim 1649.
R v Jheeta [2007] EWCA Crim 1699.
R v Morgan [1976] 2 WLR 913.
R v W & M [2010] EWCA Crim 1926.
R v Wills [2011] EWCA Crim 1938.
R v Zhang [2007] EWCA Crim 2018.

CHAPTER 2

Mapping the Theory and the Conviction Rate Attractor

Abstract This chapter presents an overview of the theoretical framework developed and deployed in the book and explores a pivotal 'attractor' that emerged from the data: conviction rates. The first section, mapping the theory, advances the book's theoretical framework through introducing key concepts in an accessible manner as possible. This enables diverse audiences, of varying levels of familiarity with the theory, to effectively engage with the book. The book's concepts are drawn from the synthesis of Deleuze's materialist philosophy of affect and sense, Deleuze and Guattari's affective assemblage theory and complexity science and theory. The final section utilises the theoretical framework to explore barristers' perspectives on the conviction rate for rape, which emerged as a key theme and 'stable attractor' in the data/assemblage. This enables us to bring the theory and data into conversation from the outset and lays the foundation for the following chapters.

Keywords New materialism and affect theory • Complex systems • Affective assemblages • Conviction rates • Barristers

A. Carline et al., *Rape and the Criminal Trial*, Palgrave Socio-Legal Studies, https://doi.org/10.1007/978-3-030-38684-9_2

2.1 Introduction

This chapter presents an overview of the theoretical framework developed and deployed in the book and explores a pivotal 'attractor' that emerged from the data, that of conviction rates. The first section, mapping the theory, advances the book's theoretical framework through introducing key concepts in an accessible manner as possible. However, a more sophisticated engagement with the theoretical framework and empirical data requires a reading of the two philosophical Chaps. 5 and 6. The key concepts in this book are drawn from the synthesis of Deleuze and Guattari's affective assemblage theory (2017, 1986, 1994, 2004), Deleuze's materialist philosophy of affect (1990, 1991, 1992) and sense and complexity science and theory (Waldrop 1992; Coveney and Highfield 1995; Kauffman 1995, 2000). This set of concepts comprises (1) two ontologies: the intensive and the actual, (2) intensive incorporeals, (3) the logic of sense, (4) the plane of composition, (5) complex systems and assemblages, (6) self-organisation and emergence, (7) phase space and high-dimensional manifolds, (8) Deleuze and Guattari's affective assemblage theory and (9) conceptualising the courtroom as an intensive affective assemblage.

The final section sets up the first engagement between the book's theoretical framework and the empirical research by focusing upon barristers' perspectives on the conviction rate for rape, which emerged as a key theme and 'stable attractor' in the data/assemblage. This enables us to bring the theory and data into conversation from the outset and lays the foundation for the following chapters.

2.2 Mapping the Theory

2.2.1 Two Ontologies: The Intensive and the Actual

Complex systems and assemblages can be understood as the co-existence and relay between two very different ontological registers: the *intensive* and the *actual*. The actual register exists extensively, that is, it is the world as we comprehend and perceive it to be. It is that which we understand and grasp as being real/existing and in this manner, it can be described as 'corporeal'. In contrast, the intensive register, while real—in that it does exist—it does so on an incorporeal or a non-physical level. The intensive register is real but not actual, whilst the extensive is both real and actual, and there is a complex and mutual relay of creation between the two. Deleuze's ontological position is that an understanding of creation and change in the extensive is unthinkable without the pre- and ongoing operation of real intensive ontological processes. The intensive register immanently creates and shapes unformed matter of expression and material organisations are brought into being and form (or actualised) in the actual register of words and things. In turn, the actualised register is surveyed and sampled by the intensive, readjusting the operations of that register accordingly. Thus, the intensive ontological register is always adjacent to every actual state of affairs and circumstance and can be intensively sensed by actual bodies in the everyday and during critical states and circumstances.

An easy way to conceptualise the incorporeal is through the notion of an atmosphere or a gaze. We know it is there, we can sense it, it can move us and we can interact with it, but we cannot physically grasp it with our hands. Thus, we can understand how the courtroom exists both actually and intensively. We can walk through the doorway, sit in the gallery, stand in the witness box, we can touch the walls—this is the 'actual corporeal courtroom'—but we can also sense and interact with it on a different level. We feel the atmospheres and emotions in the room, we can sense how they change as different bodies come and go from the actual/physical courtroom and other spaces of the courthouse (e.g. the waiting room). This is the intensive courtroom—its materiality has an incorporeal dimension. It is important to remember that the courtroom has been designed to produce certain atmospheres. For example, a sense of grandiosity, authority, tradition and hierarchy (see further Mulcahy 2011).

On this basis, what we are arguing for in this book is the existence and recognition of the incorporeal intensive courtroom: a courtroom that is *real* but not *actual*. Although not previously theorised in this way, we argue that this interpretation is intuitively understood, engaged with and embodied by courtroom actors and central to the way they approach their work. This intensive courtroom is adjacent to and generative of the actual courtroom (and vice versa), through the ongoing interactions between the two different ontological regimes. That is, the relations and processes between the different heterogeneous components from which the courtroom assemblage emerges, whilst operating within the intensive ontological register, have eventual actual outcomes in the (corpo)real world. For example, the practices barristers adopt in court, the manner in which policy and reforms are implemented (or otherwise) and the eventual jury verdict or a judge's ultimate sentence.

2.2.2 *The Intensive Incorporeals*

We can also understand the intensive and the incorporeal by focusing upon the important interactions and processes between the heterogeneous components of the system/assemblage. Both new materialism and complex theory have developed to conceptualise these dynamic interactions. From a new material perspective, we can understand them in terms of 'affects', 'sensations' and 'forces'. Affects are not reducible to emotions, although some of the literature uses those terms interchangeably. In this book, we adopt Spinoza's concept of affect which is concerned with the ability of a body (both fleshy and otherwise) to affect and be affected. By this we mean how one body interacts with another and how this interaction brings about a transformation within one or both bodies. This transformation may be positive or negative, fleeting or sustained. To quote Spinoza, 'By affect I understand affections of the Body by which the Body's power of acting is increased or decreased, aided or restrained' (Spinoza 2000: 164). This is to understand bodies as having potentialities. They are always in the process of becoming (something different), of transformation, as they interact with other bodies. We can start here to understand how giving testimony can have an intensive affect. Affects can range from the more obvious, for example, how the smell of a defendant's aftershave may produce physical and/or biological changes in the body, to the more subtle and sometimes unconscious affects, which could, for example, be linked to a change in temperature or light or the change in a tone of voice. Sensations are related to affects in that interactions between bodies may produce bodily sensations that are felt, but they may not bring about a transformation, or more specifically, an affect.

While fundamentally embodied, affect is—or can be—preconscious: it can impact upon the body without us being consciously aware of it and produce autonomic responses (Massumi 1995; Probyn 2005). While cognisance of such events often occurs, Massumi (1995) suggests that there is always an affectual excess that remains unknowable. However, this is not to assert that there is no relationship between discourse and affects. Numerous scholars illustrate how discourse (the social and cultural scripts that produce identities and meanings) and affects intertwine to produce meaning—we frequently draw upon discourses to comprehend the affects we encounter (Wetherell 2012). In addition, discourse and language can also produce affects in bodies. Indeed, cross-examination is a good example of a discourse that can negatively affect a complainant.

The courtroom can therefore be understood as involving a battle of intensive/incorporeal forces, forces that are not actual or extensive, but are the impact of affects which can be sensed. These affectual forces emanate from the various bodies at different degrees of speed and slowness, with some forces eventually overpowering others. When one affectual force prevails over another, the emerging state of the world is significantly altered. During a trial, a battle of affective forces plays out and the most forceful affect will determine what becomes actualised: that is, the guilty or not guilty verdict.

Affects, therefore, can be understood as intensive events. These events are described in philosophical literature as 'singularities' and relate to how a system operates, particularly the system's inherent capacity for radical and novel transformation. As Bonta and Protevi explain: '[s]ingularities are turning points of systems; they are "remarkable" points as opposed to "ordinary" ones … a threshold whereby a logically unique or singular pattern changes behaviour patterns' (2004: 69). Thus, these 'affect-events' bring about a qualitative transformation in the system. For example, when water reaches freezing point and becomes ice. On a basic level, we could describe the return of a verdict as a singularity. This transformation changes the nature of proceedings and a new system emerges; the defendant is sentenced or released from the justice system. However, singularities also refer to the potential of a system to transform in very radical, unexpected and non-linear ways. This could be seen in the return of a verdict that was considered unexpected, but it could also relate to reform measures bringing about unanticipated changes to the system (see Carline and Gunby 2017).

A closely allied concept within complexity theory is that of 'attractors'. Again, attractors can be used to understand how a system operates and the patterns and behaviours it adopts. These are the points towards which a system is attracted and as such, certain patterns or behaviours of a system can be seen. Guilty or not guilty are two attractors that drive the criminal justice system. However, as with singularities, there can be varied and complex attractors, which relate to the inherent potential of a system to engage in novel transformation. Two straightforward and steady types of attractors are 'state' and 'cycle' attractors. A state attractor is a stable and fixed point to which a system will tend towards. The example commonly used is of a marble in a bowl. Despite the system being agitated from time to time, the marble is persistently attracted to sitting stationary at the lowest point of the bowl. A cycle attractor explains a simple repeating system that routinely moves between two different states in a truly linear manner, for example, a pendulum. Most systems, however, while following patterns of behaviour and trajectories, do not repeat in the exact same way. This enduring pull towards particular but never quite identical configurations is known as the system's 'chaotic attractor'. The other important concept is 'basins of attraction'. Returning to our marble in the bowl, each part of the bowl leads to the lowest part of that bowl—to its stable attractor—whilst the bowl itself is the basin of attraction. However, if a significant jolt to the bowl occurred the marble could fly out and land in another bowl, with a radically different stable attractor and basin of attraction.

As we will see when exploring the data, conviction rates are a significant attractor: they frequently drive policy and law reforms. For barristers, jurors are also an attractor, driving their practices and behaviour and therefore sitting in the basin of attraction. When a system is on a point of shifting from one set of singularities (or attractors) to another, it is known as a 'bifurcation point'. At this moment, the system could shift and transform into one or another configuration or return to its previous state. A jury member being on the cusp of making a decision regarding the guilt of a defendant or a victim deciding whether or not to report an assault in the first place, can be seen as bifurcation points. Rape myths and misconceptions can be understood as attractors, and advocate questioning/trial behaviour which draws upon stereotypes related to real rape, as part of the basins of attraction.

2.2.3 A New Understanding of Sense

This approach leads us to a different conceptualisation of 'sense'. In Deleuze (1990; see also Deleuze and Guattari 1994), the intensive is lived in sensation; we sense the various affect-events, singularities and attractors. We can sense the moments, transformations and inherent potentialities of the system. This sense, however, is not to be confused with 'common' and 'good sense', which are concerned with normativity, judgement and hierarchy. Rather, sense in the intensive relates to how bodies can sense the system's incorporeals and its becomings which in turn is to 'tell the truth' of the system. This is not to say that incorporeals cannot be expressed in language, they can, and it is through sense that sensation and affects can be spoken. Hence, discourse and language can be affectual and sensational as well as representational. One way to understand this is through music and song. We recognise how songs can affect, move and transform us without physically touching us. Thus, they are not solely, if at all, about representation. We can also argue that the same applies to the testimony of a witness.

2.2.4 *The Plane of Composition*

At this juncture, it is possible to introduce the 'plane of composition', which can be distinguished from the 'plane of organisation'. The intensive regime, with all its incorporeal forces, is brought together in a consistent plane of composition. Thus, this plane is one of intensive affects and sensations (as opposed to actualisation and representation). While all that is in disequilibrium and difference is not cancelled out here, there is nevertheless a consistency to the system, known as a 'transversal consistency'. In contrast, the plane of organisation refers to the world as we know it and which can be measured by traditional scientific methodologies. Of significance to our work is that it is possible to engage with the plane of composition. We can situate ourselves within the intensive; we can excite, draw out and initiate sensations and affects. Again, a way to understand this is through music and artwork. Musicians and artists orchestrate intensive sensations and affects, as do actors. In the production of their expression they draw a plane of composition. Hence, lyrics, song, pictures, spoken words and bodily movements do more than provide a representational description devoid of emotion or feeling; rather, they embody and transmit sensation and affect. Here, we argue that barristers in the courtroom are frequently involved in drawing a plane of composition, also known as 'techniques of affect'.

2.2.5 *Complex Systems and Assemblages*

As noted in the introduction, understanding the dynamic nature of matter and the nature of affects requires a different scientific and philosophical approach, and to this end, our book turns to Deleuze and Guattari's affective assemblage theory (1986, 2004) and the underlying complex systems theory. Both a complex system and an assemblage comprise, and are the product of, the relationships and processes between many heterogeneous components—including material and immaterial bodies. The dynamics between these components, how they are connected, interact and the strengths and weakness of those interactions are the focus. These dynamic forces drive and control the system. Complex systems and assemblages can be biological (e.g. the human body) or social. Most of the social entities we know of can be described as an assemblage, for example, a town or a school. Hence, we can start to understand the court as a complex system/assemblage, in that the crucial aspect is the forces and relationships between the different components, for example, the jury, judge, barristers, solicitors, witnesses, complainants and defendants. Here, bodies also include the physical court space, where bodies are positioned, the light, the sound, the temperature and so on. It includes factors such as the law and policy, policymakers and legislatures. Understanding these relationships and the dynamic forces between them, we argue, is pivotal to understanding how the court works.

The courtroom assemblage sits within, and interacts with, other systems/assemblages and can therefore be described as 'open' and 'nested'. For example, within the courtroom assemblage sits a sexual violence assemblage, which could include rape crisis workers and Independent Sexual Violence Advisors (ISVAs) and wider policy and media constructions of rape, rape victims and perpetrators (components frequently exist in more than one assemblage and move between them). In addition, the dynamics between these heterogeneous components occur within a wider socio-economic and political context, which includes scripts of gender and sexuality, structural inequalities, rape myths, funding cuts, austerity, penal populism and agendas of neoliberal responsibilisation.

2.2.6 *Self-Organisation and Emergence*

What is fundamental to complexity theory and Deleuze and Guattari's affective assemblage theory is the possibility of the spontaneous development of novel behaviours and a new organisation of the system (1986, 2004). This is known as self-organisation, emergence, becoming and lines of flight, which means that complex systems/assemblages can operate in unpredictable and non-linear ways. While 'being' relates to the actual ontological regime, 'becoming' pertains to the intensive. In the intensive regime a system—be that an institutional system such as the criminal justice system or a biological body—is in a process of becoming as it emerges from the intensive interactions of the heterogeneous components, moving towards and between certain attractors and singularities. In this intensive state, everything is in flux and any differences and contradictions are not negated. Thus, in the intensive, a system, or a(n) (incorporeal)body, can occupy multiple conflicting states at the same time, spanning all that it can and could potentially be. So, for example, like a courtroom version of Schrodinger's cat, in the eyes of a jury a defendant may be simultaneously guilty and not guilty, until they are called upon to deliver a verdict (i.e. open the box). Similarly, witnesses may be both compelling and unconvincing in tandem. These states are known as an 'intensive superposition', with binaries being non-existent in the intensive regime. All of these intensive moments, singularities and attractors comprise the 'problem field' of a system, which co-exists alongside the 'actual problem field'. Hence, a courtroom has both an intensive (becoming) and an actual (being) problem field, which constantly interact.

2.2.7 *Phase Space or High-Dimensional Manifolds*

All the affect-events, singularities, attractors, behaviours, patterns and transformations of a system can be mapped out in 'phase-space', which can also be described as a 'graphical representation of what is occurring in the behaviour of a system' (Walker 2007: 563). This graphical representation, however, spans multi-dimensions (otherwise known as high-dimensional manifolds), which include not only time and space but all of the multifarious behaviours, patterns, tendencies and capacities of a system, including the potential for radical and novel transformation. As noted in the introduction, understanding the problem field and phase space is crucial to the production of a new materialist methodology, which is concerned with rendering perceptible, and mapping, the intensive regime.

2.2.8 *Deleuze and Guattari's Affective Assemblage Theory*

Subsequent to examining the intensive regime it is possible to set out the various elements of Deleuze and Guattari's theory of affective assemblage in more detail, in order to examine the courtroom in further depth (1986, 2004). Assemblages have a 'semiotic/expressive regime' and a 'material regime'. On a basic level, the semiotic regime comprises language and discourse, incorporating what is said in the courtroom, along with law and policy documents. In contrast, the material regime encompasses non-discursive components, such as bodies in court, the courtroom space, buildings and rooms. In reality, the semiotic and material regimes are inseparably and dynamically interconnected and interacting in affect. For example, we can see how a courtroom is both material and expressive. It exists as a building physically but also conveys a message regarding the authority of the law and is capable of producing bodily affects. The intermingling of the semiotic and material regime is a key factor when we come on to explore how the law operates within the courtroom.

Further, while assemblages come into being through processes of self-organisation and emergence, they undergo profound processes of territorialisation. Through the interactions and interconnections between heterogeneous expressive and material components, an assemblage will lay down a territory. Through processes of territorialisation, assemblages 'striate' (mark out and fix) space and constrain the very nature of the territory that can be constructed. This process not only involves the delineation of a geographical space, but also encompasses routines, customs and practices, as well as normative and dominant ways of being. Through territorialisation, assemblages construct 'codes' for bodies and social flows of production.

Coding is a top-down imposition of form and order upon bodies and behaviour emanating from, amongst other things, law and policy. As such, through striation and coding, assemblages endeavour to capture and control bodies' affects and capacities and to inhibit novel and radical transformation. Territorialisation can also be understood as a process which strives to bring about stable and repeated, and repeatable, relations between the heterogeneous components. As Tamboukou explains: 'striated spaces are hierarchical, rule-intensive, strictly bounded and confining, whereas smooth spaces are open, dynamic and allow for transformation to occur' (2008: 360). It is relatively easy to understand how a courtroom has a territory, which encompasses semiotic and material factors, including codes of law and conduct and the establishment of norms and practices. However, the territory of the courtroom is not just limited to the physical room, but is porous and expandable, incorporating, for example, judges' and barristers' chambers, solicitors' offices and the video suite at the police station, amongst other things. As there are multiple nesting and overlapping assemblages (e.g. the courtroom assemblage, the police station assemblage, the sexual violence assemblage), it is also possible to map out and examine the interaction of the different territories.

Nevertheless, territorialisation does not completely striate and code a territory. Forces of deterritorialisation run through assemblages, which are processes of destriating territories and decoding bodies and behaviours.

Indeed, deterritorialisation is an inevitable feature of territorialisation. Even if an assemblage establishes a territory that is closed, and codes and stratifies the bodies and social flows, the innate 'vitality of matter' produces forces of ceaseless creation and change. Deterritorialisation manifests in 'lines of flight', where bodies are freed from restrictions and boundaries of control. This unleashes increased capacities for affect, novel transformations and new social experimentation. However, not all deterritorialisations are entirely positive; there can be 'destroying' deterritorialisation, such as drug addiction. Nevertheless, deterritorialisation is the immanent social force that makes escape from capture and the exploration of emergence, self-organisation and novel transformation possible. These processes do not, however, enable complete freedom from the territory. Rather, deterritorialisation is followed by processes of reterritorialisation, whereby affective bodies and behaviours are recoded and territorial destriations are restriated. It is not that the operations of reterritorialisation completely undo the operation of deterritorialisation, the recoding and restriation may be substantially different to the prior striation and coding, allowing greater scope for affective production. However, a deterritorialisation that is not recuperated in some way by reterritorialisation will be rare. Thus, as opposed to being absolute, deterritorialisation will be relative and we can expect a constant relay of processes of territorialisation, deterritorialisation and reterritorialisation.

2.2.9 *Conceptualising the Courtroom as an Affective Assemblage*

With the characterisation of new materialism and the affective turn framework set out in the introduction, and the preliminary overview of key concepts of Deleuze and Guattari affective assemblage theory outlined here (1986, 2004), we can move on to conceptualise the courtroom as an affective assemblage. Conceptualising the courtroom in this way, we argue, enables a more informed and realistic understanding of courtroom dynamics and the practices of barristers. We can understand, and map out in the chapters that follow, law and policy reforms as amounting to a form of over-coding that endeavours to institute a top-down imposition of order onto practice, interacting with the established practices and customs of the courtroom. Indeed, we argue that understanding the relationship between top-down coding and courtroom practices and flows (which include all of those affect-events, attractors and singularities) is vital to comprehend the difficulties pertaining to the implementation of policies and reforms. Further, as we explore in the data, we can follow (or, in other words, map in phase space) the moments of emergence, lines of flight and de- and reterritorialisations. We can begin to build a picture of when, how and why policies and reforms are taken up in practice and the impacts they have, be those negative or positive, anticipated or otherwise and contemplate what this means for policy makers and practitioners. Further, we can begin to understand pragmatic techniques of affect that enable courtroom actors to participate and intervene in the intensive social field of the courtroom in order to compose/marshal intensive forces and make sense of (and work towards) the production of courtroom truths.

2.3 Conviction Rates: A Primary Attractor

In this section, we commence the conversation between the theory outlined and our empirical data. It is impossible to ignore the importance of conviction rates when examining the criminal justice response to rape. It forms a fundamental attractor, particularly in the development of policies and reforms, as endeavours are made to improve what has long been considered unduly low rates of conviction (Home Office 2000; Temkin and Krahe 2008; Hohl and Stanko 2015). As noted in the introduction, conviction rates have fallen markedly from 32% in 1979 to approximately 6% (Temkin and Krahe 2008; MoJ et al. 2013). There exists a significant debate within the feminist, socio-legal and criminal justice literature with respects to the construction of such rates as being 'low', and it is not our intention to repeat this here (see e.g. Stern 2010; Reece 2013; Krahe 2013; Conaghan and Russell 2014). Nevertheless, conviction rates have been identified by numerous bodies, including the government as well as researchers, as a particular issue within the problem field of the rape courtroom affective assemblage. Hence, our focus here is to maintain the political agenda of the existing feminist and critical critiques, but to re-energise the debate by exploring the problematic through a novel theoretical framework. From this perspective, understanding the importance of conviction rates is vital to mapping the problem field, phase space and the flows of affects and sensations, because from the perspective of policy makers and legislatures, improving the system equals improving the number of convictions achieved.

The potential for a conviction is a vital factor considered at key decision-making points within the justice system and can therefore be situated as a singularity which can shift a system from a bifurcation point. For example, when deciding whether to prosecute a case the CPS will determine whether there is a realistic chance of conviction (CPS 2018). At this point, however, various attractors and their related basins will come into play, including, for example, understandings of the jury and their past decision-making processes, concerns regarding myths and the absence or otherwise of independent and forensic evidence (see Carline and Gunby 2017, 2019). As is well known, there is divergence regarding how rates of conviction should be calculated (Stern 2010). If that rate is based on the number of cases reported to the police, it remains at about 5%–6% and has done since the early 2000s. In contrast, some have argued that the rate should be recalculated based on just those cases which are prosecuted. In adopting this model, around 50%–60% of cases result in a conviction (Stern 2010). The latter approach clearly presents a more positive account of the system, but obstructs a more holistic understanding of criminal justice processes, vital bifurcation points, feedback and interaction between trial outcomes and CPS decision-making (see further Carline and Gunby 2019).

Barristers were divided on the topic of whether there was a problem with the rape conviction rate. Around a third argued that the rate was too low, half disagreed with this perspective and the remaining minority were uncertain. Barristers were unequivocal in their views in each direction. For example, barrister 33 (male, hereafter B33M) was convinced that there were too many acquittals, despite B9F stating that the contention that the rate was too low was inaccurate and 'leaves a very bad taste in my mouth'. Others argued that it was 'irresponsible to pedal the myth that the conviction rate's really low' (B10F) because this puts 'people off reporting', portrays the system in an inadequate light and undermines the jury 'which undermines the system fundamentally' (B23M). Barristers were keen to maintain the integrity of the system they worked within and understood that discourses around low rates of conviction could have an affectual force on the decision-making processes of victims (see e.g. Prochuk 2018). However, a line of flight emerged here whereby discomfort was expressed by a minority of advocates around questionable trial outcomes and their relationship with conviction rates: 'Sometimes you get an acquittal and you're pretty certain that they have [committed the offence]. And that's not a comfortable place to be' (B12F). Similarly, B38M commented:

> [Y]ou've got to, as a society, accept that you've got lots of people that have been sexually abused … and juries have not convicted the [perpetrators]. That's a huge thing to accept for me.

Thus, in a system that prioritises conviction outcomes, through these perspectives we can also start to render perceptible and map the affects that working on rape cases can precipitate in advocates (see Gunby and Carline 2019 for a detailed discussion). They also point to the emergence of an intensive superposition, whereby when defending barristers must marshal affects and sensations that convey to the jury their client's innocence—even if thinking (or suspecting) otherwise. Hence, in the context of their role, advocates must occupy the conflicting state of assuming that their client is innocent and guilty, spanning all that the accused can and potentially could be.

Despite half of advocates maintaining that there was not a problem with conviction rates, a significant number still acknowledged that they had prosecuted cases in which the jury's decision to acquit was 'absurd' (B22M), 'actually perverse' (B14F) and 'a really odd result' (B27F). Although barristers are privy to evidence that jurors will never see, and this may contextualise their perspectives, it was noted that 'there are some surprising results' and typically, these would be 'surprising acquittals' (B35M). Here then, we can begin to see the non-linear reality of the courtroom assemblage and the ability for an outcome to emerge which was unforeseen; an outcome which can cause tensions for barristers and keep conviction rates low. As such, it was noted that it was 'very important to convey to … complainants … that it is a lottery' (B16F). This led two barristers to note that it was frequently not possible to 'predict what a verdict would be' (B35M) and that '[l]awyers are really bad at reading juries' (B13M). Hence, whilst barristers do develop an intensive sense of the system (as we come on the analyse), and could for the most part 'tell from the reaction you get from a jury as to whether or not something struck home' (B21F), the space for emergence and self-organisation in the form of unexpected jury decisions remains, which renders intuiting trial outcomes difficult.

Despite the differing views regarding the rate of conviction, connecting threads emerged around the challenges in obtaining said convictions, which we can map as attractors and their corresponding basins of attraction in phase space. The first attractor concerned the need for corroborating evidence, with the majority of participants emphasising the high threshold for a guilty verdict and the frequent perceived lack of supporting/independent evidence. For example, those who felt there was a problem with conviction rates argued that 'rapes are harder to prove' (B34M) due to that lack of supporting evidence. Similarly, B7F stated that 'where you have one person's word against another, in any case … you are always going to have a lower conviction rate'. It was noted that the presence of forensics or some other form of independent evidence would help the jury feel 'comforted' (B31F) and as such, barristers had a feel that juries 'are looking for some, you know, extra outside piece of evidence which is gonna clinch it for them' (B3M). However, jurors' expectations regarding the need for forensic or 'additional' evidence to establish the proof of non-consensual sex could be seen to map on to stereotypes regarding 'real rape'. For example, that the victim will have suffered physical injuries, despite forensic evidence being rare and typically unequivocal in rape cases (Sommers and Baskin 2011).

Furthermore, in line with research (Ellison and Munro 2010), barristers perceived that 'juries will apply a higher level of proof' (B37F) in rape cases and that unless they were 'absolutely a hundred percent sure' (B31F) they would not convict. This application of a higher burden can therefore be pinpointed as a second attractor related to conviction rates. In addition, just under a quarter of participants expressed the opinion that juries were reluctant to convict in the absence of evidence, due to the stigma and labelling associated with a rape conviction (see Ellison and Munro 2010; Gunby et al. 2012), signalling the existence of a third attractor:

> I think it's just because the offending is so serious and the label is such a huge label to carry, um, I think it does weigh really, really heavily with jurors. … I think it makes for a very difficult decision-making process for them. (B8F)

There was, however, disagreement regarding the jury's perception of what constituted evidence. B35M stated that it was disappointing that juries will often request 'concrete evidence' or argue that 'there is no evidence', failing to recognise that 'somebody's word' is sufficient. The concerns around, and construction of what amounts to independent and verifiable evidence, can therefore be positioned as a stable attractor in the system and one which we return to in the discussion of courtroom performances. There is undoubtedly a significant relevant legal history which has impacted upon the stability of this attractor, given the previous evidential requirements regarding corroboration and the relevance of an early complainant (see further Temkin 2002; Carline and Easteal 2014).

2.4 Conclusion

Through barristers' perspectives on conviction rates, we can start to map attractors and their basins in phase space and understand how they impact and drive a system. In turn, we can start to appreciate the challenges this poses for introducing change into that system. As we will see when we discuss the data in further depth, barristers' perspectives on the perceived lack of independent evidence informed their views on the importance of various courtroom expressions and performances and the affects they tried to marshal as part of their practice.

References

Bonta, M., & Protevi, J. (2004). *Deleuze and Geophilosophy: A Guide and Glossary.* Edinburgh: Edinburgh University Press.

Carline, A., & Easteal, P. (2014). *Shades of Grey – Domestic and Sexual Violence Against Women: Law Reform and Society.* Abingdon: Routledge.

Carline, A., & Gunby, C. (2017). Rape Politics, Policies and Practice: Exploring the Tensions and Unanticipated Consequences of Well-Intended Victim-Focused Measures. *The Howard Journal, 56*, 34–52.

Carline, A., & Gunby, C. (2019). Justice for Rape Complainants: Limitations and Possibilities. In P. Carlen & L. A. Franca (Eds.), *Justice Alternatives* (pp. 306–320). Abingdon: Routledge.

Conaghan, J., & Russell, Y. (2014). Rape Myths, Law and Feminist Research: 'Myths About Myths'. *Feminist Legal Studies, 22*(1), 25–48.

Coveney, P., & Highfield, R. (1995). *Frontiers of Complexity: The Search for Order in a Chaotic World.* London: Faber and Faber.

Crown Prosecution Service (CPS). (2018). *The Code for Crown Prosecutors.* Retrieved from https://www.cps.gov.uk/publication/code-crown-prosecutors.

Deleuze, G. (1990). *Logic of Sense.* London: Athlone Press.

Deleuze, G. (1991). *Bergsonism.* New York: Zone Books.

Deleuze, G. (1992). *Expressionism in Philosophy: Spinoza.* New York: Zone Books.

Deleuze, G., & Guattari, F. (1986). *Kafka: Toward a Minor Literature.* Minneapolis: University of Minnesota Press.

Deleuze, G., & Guattari, F. (1994). *What Is Philosophy?* London: Verso.

Deleuze, G., & Guattari, F. (2004). *A Thousand Plateaus.* London: Continuum.

Deleuze, G., & Guattari, F. (2017). *Anti-Oedipus.* London: Bloomsbury.

Ellison, L., & Munro, V. E. (2010). Getting to (Not) Guilty: Examining Jurors' Deliberative Processes in and Beyond the Context of a Mock Rape Trial. *Legal Studies, 30*(1), 74–97.

Gunby, C., Carline, A., & Beynon, C. (2012). Regretting It After? Perspectives on Alcohol Consumption, Nonconsensual Sex and False Allegations of Rape. *Social and Legal Studies, 22*(1), 87–106.

Hohl, K., & Stanko, B. (2015). Complaints of Rape and the Criminal Justice System: Fresh Evidence on the Attrition Problem in England and Wales. *European Journal of Criminology, 12*(3), 324–341.

Home Office. (2000). *Setting the Boundaries: Reforming the Law on Sex Offences* (Vol. 1). London: Home Office.

Kauffman, S. (1995). *At Home in the Universe: The Search for Laws of Self-Organisation and Complexity.* Oxford: Oxford University Press.

Kauffman, S. (2000). *Investigations.* Oxford: Oxford University Press.

Krahe, B. (2013). *Myths About Myths? Let the Evidence Speak. A Common on Reece.* Retrieved from https://www.uni-potsdam.de/fileadmin01/projects/sozial-psychologie/images/pdf/Comment_Reece_Paper.pdf.

Ministry of Justice (MoJ), Home Office, and Office for National Statistics (ONS). (2013). *An Overview of Sexual Offending in England and Wales.* London: Ministry of Justice, Home Office, and ONS.

Massumi, B. (1995). The Autonomy of Affect. *Cultural Critique Part, 31*(II), 83–109.

Mulcahy, L. (2011). *Legal Architecture: Justice, Due Process and the Place of Law.* Abingdon: Routledge.

Probyn, E. (2005). *Blush: Faces of Shame.* Minnesota: University of Minnesota Press.

Prochuk, A. (2018). *We Are Here: Women's Experiences of the Barriers to Reporting Sexual Assault.* Vancouver: West Coast Leaf.

Reece, H. (2013). Rape Myths: Is Elite Opinion Right and Popular Opinion Wrong? *Oxford Journal of Legal Studies, 33*(3), 445–473.

Sommers, I., & Baskin, D. (2011). The Influence of Forensic Evidence on the Case Outcomes of Rape Incidents. *The Justice System Journal, 32*(3), 314–334.

Spinoza, B. (2000). *Ethics.* Oxford: Oxford University Press.

Stern Review. (2010). *A Report by Baroness Vivien Stern CBE of an Independent Review into How Rape Complaints Are Handled by Public Authorities in England and Wales.* London: Home Office.

Tamboukou, M. (2008). Machinic Assemblages: Women, Art Education and Space. *Discourse, 29*(3), 359–375.

Temkin, J. (2002). *Rape and the Legal Process.* Oxford: Oxford University Press.

Temkin, J., & Krahe, B. (2008). *Sexual Assault and the Justice Gap: A Question of Attitude.* Oxford: Hart Publishing.

Waldrop, M. (1992). *Complexity: The Emerging Science at the Edge of Order and Chaos.* Simon and Schuster.

Walker, J. T. (2007). Advancing Science and Research in Criminal Justice/ Criminology: Complex Systems Theory and Non-Linear Analyses. *Justice Quarterly, 24*(4), 555–581.

Wetherell, M. (2012). *Affect and Emotion: A New Social Science Understanding*. London: Sage Publications.

CHAPTER 3

Courtroom Expressions: The Intermingling of the Semiotic and Material Regimes

Abstract In this chapter, we begin to explore the courtroom affective assemblage, by focusing specifically, although not exclusively, upon the semiotic regime, as it relates to the offence of rape. By exploring barristers' perspectives, we gain original insight into how the system works and the factors that enable or inhibit the implementation of sexual offence law reforms and policy. This allows us to explore the processes and interactions between different components within the assemblage, to map their patterns, flows and outcomes and begin to make them visible. Of significance is how the law plays out in practice, how it is implemented through the interactive processes between heterogeneous components and moments of self-organisation and emergence. We note how barristers expressed a preference for smooth over striated space and for provisions/reforms produced by those who have an 'intensive sense' of the courtroom.

Keywords Courtroom assemblage • Semiotic regime • *Sexual Offences Act 2003* • Rape policies • Myths • Intensive sense

A. Carline et al., *Rape and the Criminal Trial*, Palgrave Socio-Legal Studies, https://doi.org/10.1007/978-3-030-38684-9_3

3.1 Introduction

In this chapter, we begin to explore the courtroom affective assemblage, by focusing specifically, although not exclusively, upon the semiotic/expressive regime as it relates to the offence of rape. By exploring barristers' perspectives, we can gain insight into how the system works and the factors that enable or inhibit the implementation of sexual offence law reforms and policy. This allows us to explore the processes and interactions between different components within the assemblage, to map their patterns, flows and outcomes. What is significant here is how the law plays out in practice, how it is implemented through the interactive processes between heterogeneous components and moments of self-organisation and emergence. This involves developing an understanding of, and mapping, the various affect-events, singularities and attractors which drive the system.

Given the expansive legal and policy framework that exists in relation to rape, it is not possible to provide an overview of the entire semiotic regime. That would be a considerable undertaking beyond the scope of this project. Accordingly, we structure the analysis by focusing upon the higher order themes that emerged from the data. The first: 'reflections on the legal semiotic regime' includes the lower order themes of 'consent definition: s.74', 'mens rea: reasonable belief in consent', 'evidential and conclusive presumptions: s.75 and s.76' and 'legislation and convictions rates'. The second higher order theme: 'the affectual force of the mistaken assumptions directions' includes the lower order theme of 'defence counsel, myths and reterritorialisation', whilst the final overarching theme is entitled: 'intensive sense: policies, practice and experience'.

3.2 Reflections on the Legal Semiotic Regime

An easy starting point for exploring the territory of the rape courtroom assemblage is to commence with the key pieces of legislation. These are part of the semiotic regime and can be understood as top-down coding within the territory; legislators and policymakers create them, and practitioners are expected to adopt them. For our purposes, the *Sexual Offences Act 2003* is a vital aspect of the semiotic regime, which has been subjected to revisions and interpretation by the superior courts. In addition, there is a plethora of policies, toolkits and judicial directions which can likewise be situated in the semiotic regime. The intention here is not to provide a doctrinal critique of the key provisions, but to begin to explore how these elements of the semiotic operate in practice. In addition, it will start to shed light on some of the key stable attractors in the system.

We can conceptualise the substantive law as an over-coding, it is a top-down imposition of order within an assemblage. Of importance is the distinction between striated space (hierarchical, rule-intensive and confining) and smooth space (open, dynamic and supportive of transformation). From a legal doctrinal perspective, top-down coding endeavours to striate: the letter of the law is to be applied. However, this blocks moments of self-organisation and emergence. The manner in which barristers talked about the law demonstrates that they adopt a very different semiotic regime to that of the legal/doctrinal approach. There is a merging of the semiotic and material regimes in the courtroom assemblage which rallies against this over-coding and striation. Indeed, fundamental to a barrister's use and application of the law is their intensive sense of how a rape trial operates. Barristers' sense of the role and significance of discourse/expression in the courtroom is that it is there to produce affects, to create sensation and (intensive) sense—namely, to move bodies. This is a key attractor that drives the system, but one that sits in conflict with the striated nature of legislative over-coding. Barristers tended to be supportive of substantive law when it conformed to their ability to engage in techniques of affect, which requires smooth space.

In this manner, we can begin to understand how barristers are engaged in drawing a plane of composition, which sits in contrast with the plane of organisation that tends to correspond with the development of legislation. As such, it is vital that this factor is taken into consideration when developing legislative and policy measures. Indeed, the substantive criminal law was argued by over two-thirds of the sample to have little to do with rape trials and was frequently constructed as irrelevant. It was stated that 'you can't legislate for human behaviour' (B19M) and that various provisions have not 'made any material difference' (B25F) because of their perceived inability to engage with the intensive realities of the courtroom. However, the extent to which various elements of the 2003 Act were deemed useful, and the degree to which they were used, depended upon on the specific provision, as we outline.

3.2.1 Consent Definition: s.74

In a rape case the victim's consent, or the lack thereof, is the pivotal issue. Thus, we can start to structure consent as another key attractor and a decision as to whether or not the victim consented, a bifurcation point and a vital singularity. Given the pivotal importance of consent, it is perhaps not surprising that almost all barristers supported the introduction of a statutory definition on the basis that it was 'helpful for the jury to have that very clear ... definition' (B9F). It was noted that consent was not 'universally understood' (B20M) and was 'a difficult issue' (B17F). As such, s.74 proved useful as 'it provides guidance for the juries [and] ... they're the most important people in a trial' (B8F). The jury is undoubtedly a key attractor in the courtroom assemblage and this was also a critical lens through which barristers assessed (and supported or rejected) legal developments. If developments were perceived to be helpful/useful to the jury, barristers expressed support for the provision. These perspectives emphasise the important dynamic interconnection between barristers and the jury, with it being striking to see them referred to as the 'most important people in a trial', over and above the complainant and defendant whose conflict it is. Thus, this is the barrister's sense of the problem field in the courtroom, its attractors and singularities and this sense becomes the truth of the trial and pivotal to how cases are approached. Here, we can trace the significant intermingling of the semiotic and material regimes where for advocates, the importance of expression in the courtroom flows from its ability to affect the jury. We return to this point throughout the chapter and Chap. 4.

However, around a quarter of barristers focused more specifically upon the importance of the judge's directions in relation to consent, as opposed to the definition itself, and this also becomes a key attractor which can be mapped throughout the rape courtroom assemblage. This leads us to consider the importance of the interactions between the judge and the jury and sheds light on the position of the judge more generally within the courtroom assemblage. The data frequently attested to the affectual pull of the judge. It was noted that 'it all comes down to the judge's written direction' (B13M) and that while 'it's fascinating to have a legal debate about what consent is' what really matters is how 'the judge directs the jury as to the meaning of consent' (B34M). As such, the judge was frequently positioned as more significant than the codes produced by parliament. Through this, we can see the regard barristers place on bottom-up developments, as opposed to the imposition of top-down over-coding which could be resisted unless it corresponded with barristers' sense of the problem field of the courtroom.

A significant minority of participants, however, expressed concern that the consent definition had 'made it more complicated' (B12F), leading them to adopt a more critical perspective. Once again, this view flowed from their consideration of whether the definition would be useful to the jury. These barristers argued that the definition had not made any practical difference because 'I think jurors fundamentally get consent' (B24F). However, this assumption tended to be discussed in terms of common sense, as opposed to intensive sense (the latter being focused on how bodies can sense the system's incorporeals and becomings whilst the former concerns normativity, judgement and hierarchy). As B36M argued: 'I think jurors use common sense'. These perspectives do not sit comfortably with evidence that indicates sexual consent 'literacy' is not a given (Beres 2010; Gunby et al. 2012; Muehlenhard et al. 2016; Carline et al. 2018). However, what we can start to see here is a conflict between common sense and intensive sense, a tension that barristers battled with and where we see the interaction between the intensive and the actual registers. While the techniques of affect and plane of composition that barristers engaged in are concerned with producing intensive sense, namely, discourses and expressions which provoke affects, barristers would frequently revert to normative notions of common sense, which belong to the realm of representation.

A third perspective developed points to the reality of self-organisation and emergence within the system. Corresponding with existing research (Finch and Munro 2006; Gunby et al. 2010; Carline and Gunby 2011), a significant minority of barristers argued that jurors would not concern themselves with a statutory definition but would instead apply their own understanding. At times, this was linked to the juror's perceived inability to understand consent: 'I don't get the feeling from jurors that they grasp the concept immediately. ... There's a risk that if they don't understand it they will do their own thing' (B20M). Hence, in contrast to those views expressed above, at times, it was felt that jurors misunderstood the legal meaning of consent. Such distinct views likely point to the non-linear nature of the system, whereby differently constituted juries may emit different sensations regarding their understanding of the law. It also suggests that certain barristers get an intensive sense—a feel—for what works with jurors and informs their views on the semiotic regime accordingly. Perhaps more strikingly, this self-organisation and emergence could take place even if the law was understood: 'regardless of what the law is, I think a jury makes its own mind up on what consent is' (B6F). This could thus be seen as a line of flight as it amounts to an effective decoding. That is, the jury resists the definition of consent set down by the legislature and apply their own understanding. Hence, there always remains a potential non-linearity within the courtroom, where law is decoded and space de-striated. Barristers' perspectives here were not generated via engaging in research with juries, but flow from their feel and sense of the courtroom. They have a sense of affect-events, attractors and singularities and it is these sensations that drive their practice and acceptance (or otherwise) of law reforms and policies.

While many expressed support for s.74, because it was thought to be helpful for the jury, this did not mean that the definition was thought to have impacted trials. Overall, the definition was considered to be fairly inconsequential: 'in practice, I don't think it's made a jot of difference' (B19M) and while it might be 'useful in the sense that it gave us a code … it hasn't … impacted in the way people hoped it might' (B21F). Further, it was clear that the definition of consent was not a key factor in barristers' techniques of affect. In contrast, what mattered was the competing affectual pull of competing testimonies: 'it's not so much a legal definition, it's which version of the facts do you accept' (B37M). As such, while consent was a significant attractor and singularity during the trial, its force was not related to the legal definition, but rather with respect to developing an affective account of what happened:

> [Consent] would probably be the centre of my whole speech, but it won't be the law that's at the centre of my whole speech in terms of what consent actually is, [instead] what this person did to indicate that she was consenting; or what she didn't do … you know … the sort of non-spoken things, or the failing to do anything at all. (B6F)

As such, while the definition of consent was typically considered common sense, this did not mean that it had intensive sense. Namely, sense that could bring about a significant transformation, move the jury and resolve a bifurcation point, that is, guilty/not guilty. While we can see that the substantive law is part of the semiotic regime of the assemblage, what is significant is not the letter of the law, but the affectual force of discourse and expression. As such, we see a crucial intermingling of the semiotic and material regimes.

3.2.2 *Mens Rea: Reasonable Belief in Consent*

The adoption of an objective test was unanimously supported by advocates who argued that the move more effectively held defendants to account for their conduct. It was stated that 'you've got to bring in that ... degree of objectivity' (B3M). As with consent, the key attractor for barristers regarding their reception to the reform was the jury. It was felt that the objective test had made the law 'much easier for [the jury] to get their heads round' (B31F). It was also considered to be 'old fashioned to be saying to the jury ... the defendant genuinely thought that his advances would be welcome ... if the person was saying no or turning away' (B17F). This was seen to reflect developments in sexual attitudes and behaviour:

> Blokes used to be able to stand up in court and just say ... she'd said yes before. But now ... it doesn't matter whether she said yes before, it doesn't matter whether she's going to say yes tomorrow, it's on this particular occasion. (B15F)

This perspective implicates a line of flight away from dominant discourses pertaining to female sexuality and availability. It shows the potential for law to embody change and engage in (relative) processes of deterritorialisation, which were recognised and seized upon by barristers. The change in mens rea was also argued to prevent the defence from running outlandish arguments: 'as the prosecutor, you can say, well, you may believe the defendant ... and he may be telling the truth but his ... defence is utterly absurd' (B1M)—perspectives that resonate with academic commentary emphasising the symbolic importance of the objective test (Cowan 2007). Here then, we can see the approval of a provision on the basis that it chimes with appropriate societal notions of sexual intimacy and would play well with the jury. However, at the same time, it was noted that the jury raised questions as to the definition of 'reasonable', implicating that its scope may be unduly broad (Ellison and Munro 2013; Larcombe et al. 2016).

As with consent, certain advocates referred to common sense when stating their approval of an objective/reasonableness test. Indeed, the requirement that a defendant's belief should be reasonable in the circumstances was considered 'utterly sensible' (B1M). However, when we map what this notion of sense means in the courtroom, it becomes clear that the more progressive views on sexual behaviour outlined were subject to considerable reterritorialisation. In other words, despite the provision aiming to dispel myths, these were frequently drawn on to deduce reasonableness. For example, B30M noted that '[a]ll you have to do is have a few signals, well, she gave me her number, well, we were flirting, yes, we had a dance ... she came back to my house'. Hence, while a positive line of flight emerged regarding the potential of the objective test to challenge problematic assumptions, in practice, this can be easily reterritorialised and brought back into heteronormative scripts.

Despite advocates being supportive of the reform, they were nevertheless critical of the focus on 'the steps taken' to ascertain consent. It was argued that this did not capture the nuances of sexual interactions in 'the real world' (B8F) and in turn, the statutory language did not correspond with how individuals identify consent or culpability in rape cases (Larcombe et al. 2016). It was argued that people would 'find it particularly bizarre ... that during sexual conduct of any description, you would pause and go, just so that I'm clear, how do you feel about the sexual activity' (B31F). Thus, on this basis, the steps were considered a 'red herring' (B2M) and made 'a mockery' (B37F) of juries' understandings and experience of life. Here then, we see the attractor of 'real life' emerge and a conflict between how life and legal provisions are sensed and unfold in the courtroom assemblage, navigated by advocates and over-coded by legislatures. This, in turn, impacted upon the extent to which the provision was used: 'I don't, in practice, think that sort of questioning is particularly ... asked' (B3M). From a defence perspective, asking a defendant to clarify what steps he had taken to ascertain consent was also considered counterproductive: 'he's interested in getting off and I'm going to get him or her off. And they [the jury] don't like engaging in intellectual argument' (B15F). Indeed, the 'intellectual', representational provision was considered too far removed from the intensive plane of composition/techniques of affect that advocates strive to marshal in the courtroom. As with consent, it was felt that juries would apply their own understandings, again opening up space for self-organisation and emergence.

3.2.3 Evidential and Conclusive Presumptions: s.75 and s.76

A Home Office (2006) stocktake of the 2003 Act demonstrated that the presumptions had not had the impact anticipated, a finding replicated in our data (also see Gunby et al. 2010; Carline and Gunby 2011, 2017). Barristers were unanimous in their agreement that the presumptions were rarely, if ever used, and this represents one of the clearest examples of decoding within the courtroom assemblage. Once again, the jury attractor was a key explanation as to why the presumptions were not utilised. However, it was also noted that they were not supported by judges. When working through advocates' perspectives, we again see the emergence of the attractor of common sense, along with the attractors of over-complicating the trial and the reality of practice. These frequently inter-linked and provide key insights into the implementation, or otherwise, of related provisions.

Almost all barristers argued that the presumptions were not used, that they were not 'particularly helpful' (B3M), that they were 'a bit patronising' (B31F) and 'common sense' (B9F). In exploring the attractor of common sense specifically, barristers were keen to assert that the situations covered by the presumptions represented areas where intuitively there would be no consent: 'if someone's unconscious and you can prove that, they're obviously not consenting' (B29M). As such, they were typically constructed as an unnecessary addition. In contrast, barristers would adopt a 'fairly pragmatic and practice [based] view' (B27F), which meant building the case on the basis of the evidence. Again, we see a focus on the affectual force of evidence, as opposed to the striating effect of the letter of the law, with the latter being considered to add nothing of value to the material affect of evidence: 'now the reality is for a jury, how likely are you to [consent after being violently assaulted?] So it becomes part of the evidence, which is powerful evidence' (B33M). This led to reflection on the reality of courtroom practice, with it being argued that the presumptions were not used because they simply codified existing approaches: 'it just puts into practice what was probably being done anyway' (B26F)—again pointing to the importance of, and preference for, bottom-up emergence.

Again, we see that if legislation is considered to do nothing to assist a case, and the barrister's ability to affect the jury, it will be side-lined by counsel. Mapping this movement and decoding sheds light onto advocates' receptivity to new legislation and legislators and policy makers must develop a keener sense (an intensive sense) of what occurs in the courtroom in order to inform implementation: 'it's all very well writing … the laws like that, but if they don't actually … work out that way in real cases, then they're not worth having' (B2M). Laws that were intended to bring about a significant transformation—institute a singularity—could struggle in their attempt if advocates considered them to be at odds with or an unnecessary addition to, their everyday practice and interaction with the jury. Our data shows a significant resistance to over-coding generated by individuals who were perceived to lack an understanding of the courtroom reality, or in our language, the incorporeal trial.

A further attractor developed around the implementation of the law, which again concentrated on the jury, was that of 'over complication'. Around two-thirds of barristers argued that the presumptions made what was in many ways a simple matter overly complicated and this 'causes all manner of problems' (B13M). Barristers reported that this concern was shared by judges, who then fostered a culture and practice of non-implementation. It was noted that judges and barrister both 'shy away from them' because they do not make 'matters much clearer for the jury' (B26F) and that the use of the presumption would be confusing and ultimately, 'you'll lose a juror' (B2M). Here, we can see a concern with the negative affects of the semiotic regime; losing a juror would impact negatively on the techniques of affect barristers attempted to marshal in court and this view was purportedly shared by judges. Hence, a mutual intensive sense amongst practitioners regarding the best operation of the system could be seen, with this guiding practice accordingly. Further evidence of self-organisation, emergence and practitioners' intensive sense driving court practices could be seen in response to those cases that fell within the scope of the presumptions. Advocates noted that the defence and prosecutor would collectively produce a suitable direction for those cases: 'I think more often than not, the lawyers between them manage to come [up] with a form of word[ing] for judicial directions which deal with these issues' (B34M). Overall, it was argued that 'whether you're defending or prosecuting … simple is best' (B38M), pointing again to a preference for smooth space, developing a plane of composition and engaging in techniques of affect. Complicated law could confuse the jury and potentially detract from an affectual pull.

Concerns regarding complexity were not limited to the presumptions, with it being overwhelmingly agreed that rape law generally bored jurors, could result in them 'switching off' and 'glazing over' (B20M). It was argued that 'jury trials tend to work best with evidence and as little law as possible' (B35M). A key attractor, therefore, was the desire to keep the trial simple and focus on the disputed facts, as opposed to legal definitions. This again points to the desire for smooth space, which allows for affects, sensations and emergence, as opposed to a rule-bounded and restricted striated space which prohibits flows and forces. The effort to manage this complexity, make things comprehensible and to foster a smoother space could be seen in the account of B33M. They discussed a case in which they negotiated for two hours with opposing counsel for a suitably translatable version of the law which they could give to the jury to help them interpret the legalities at hand. This, again, shows the bottom-up emergence that frequently occurs during the trial, whereby the directions that the judge provides are a product of the interactions between counsel. This advocate also reflected:

> Now, if it takes us two hours to arrive at the question with our collective sixty, seventy years of experience in law behind us, how easy is it for them as laymen to interpret and especially—not just interpret—but use that law on a set of circumstances? (B33M)

Thus, juries are not perceived to be concerned with interpreting the (semiotic) law, but rather putting it to work to help determine facts within the material regime/circumstances.

3.2.4 *Legislation and Conviction Rates*

In light of these discussions, we can start to map a scepticism regarding the utility of reforms and it was clear that provisions tended not to operate in practice as initially conceived. Over two-thirds of the sample argued that rape legislation was ineffectual: 'no matter how much you legislate, things remain very much the same' (B21F), a sentiment that resonates closely with Cook's (2011) work. This was particularly the case in terms of conviction rates. While the driving force of improving convictions was recognised to be the catalyst for the reforms discussed, this had not played out in practice: 'I don't think [they've] helped the conviction rates' (B30M), remarks supported by evidence (Hohl and Stanko 2015). As such, while the 2003 Act was a 'nice political idea' (B31F), it did not make 'any material difference' (B25F) when 'at the sharp end in front of a jury' (B21F). Thus, we can arguably see a clash of territories between penal populism (the political agenda to increase conviction rates, which frequently drives reform endeavours) and the courtroom assemblage (the way law operates/is utilised in trials). The former does not complement the latter and following this line of argument enables us to develop a better understanding of the implementation gap. Barristers were consistent in their perspectives that what counted was the affectual pull of evidence, as opposed to the letter of the law. Over-coding was seen as trying to striate patterns of behaviour in order to produce a conviction, clashing with the reality of the courtroom which involves a battle of affective forces and the production of sense:

> This is all an attempt to get more convictions, right? It doesn't make any difference at all. If they're sure what she's saying is true, he'll be convicted. If they're not sure, he'll be acquitted, no matter what legislation you pass. (B33M)

All of this analysis renders perceptible the operation of the system, the reality of the interactions between heterogeneous components, emergence and non-linearity. Bodies (i.e. judges and barristers) within the courtroom, who have a sense of the system, react to over-coding, resisting those reforms which counteract their understanding of how the system operates. This could be seen in advocates' reflections on who has the experience and legitimacy to develop appropriate provisions: 'people who put these codes in place … they're not drafted by people who actually have to stand up there and speak to twelve people about this' (B21F). As noted, there was a preference for solutions inherent and emergent within the system, with B24F noting: 'I think that rape is tried very differently and has been over the last ten years, but that's as a result of a number … of Court of Appeal decisions'. Decisions made by higher courts, or those with the same intensive sense of the system, perhaps unsurprisingly, received greater support.

What also flowed from the data was the sense that changes within the system, particularly in relation to responses to sexual violence complainants, stemmed from wider cultural and societal shifts, as opposed to statute: 'I think the main improvements have been cultural rather than statute based' (B34M) and 'what needed to happen is what has happened, which is a cultural shift in how we approach things, how we perceive things … and how we deal with victims of such sensitive crimes' (B27F). We can therefore see here how the system interacts with, and responds to, wider issues and assemblages, particularly sexual violence and victimhood assemblages. Hence, it was argued that despite the good intentions of legislature and policy makers, the imposition of new provisions and substantive legislative over-coding was not the solution to the problem of low conviction rates. The lack of positive outcome in this regard led to the suggestion that some form of pre-testing of provisions might have been useful. 'Um, but they don't test run these changes in legislation, do they? I mean, I don't know how you can test run it, but I don't think it's been a great success' (B26F). This idea of 'pre-testing' relates to the concept of adaptive management, which we explore in the conclusion, and the importance of ongoing feedback loops within the system to enable the proliferation of more productive solutions. It also relates to the problem field—where we find all potential problems (and solutions)—and the interaction between the intensive and actual, where the former samples the latter and the problem field shifts in consequence. Thus, there must be detailed consideration on how best to initiate and implement reform provisions, a point to which we return.

3.3 The Affectual Force of the Mistaken Assumptions Directions

In addition to the 2003 Act, we can situate the 'mistaken assumptions' directions (Judicial College 2019) as part of the semiotic regime of the courtroom assemblage. In terms of our theory, myths and misconceptions relating to rape and sexual violence can be situated as a relatively stable singularity and basin of attraction which have significant sway upon the courtroom assemblage (and other wider assemblages). Understanding them in this way sheds light on their entrenched nature, making them so difficult to shift. We can view myths as part of the code or dominant discourse which emerges within a territory, linked to molar, or macro and dominant notions of female sexuality, which are fundamentally negative in their affects. That is, they prevent the flourishing of life. In this context, we can understand the mistaken assumption directions as a deterritorialisation, due to their potential to disrupt problematic dominant/molar scripts and discourses.

Almost all barristers in our sample spoke favourable about these 'myth-busting' directions (see Temkin 2010; Temkin et al. 2018; Smith and Skinner 2017 for a discussion of the sometimes inadequate or absent use of them). Whilst barristers would themselves draw on myths, particularly when defending (a tension we come on to explore), the directions were, on the face of things, considered 'fantastic' (B4F), 'very powerful' (B11M) and 'the very best innovation that there's been' (B5F), because myths should not be allowed to influence courtroom practices. Over three-quarters of the sample believed that the directions impacted upon a trial and were 'massively influential' (B12F) with respect to convictions and acquittals. One barrister surmised that they had 'absolutely no doubt that those judges that give [the directions] better prominence' (B4F) had a higher conviction rate, an assumption implicated in other work (Temkin et al. 2018), even if not evidenced in official statistics.

The directions were said to 'reflect real life and human psychology' (B10F) and appropriately inform the jury that 'there is no such thing as a standard rape victim' (B25F). It was argued that the directions were important as 'juries do need to be told, as we know, they do hold these myths' (B4F). As such, they were seen to play an important educative function in that they aimed to give the jury 'that sort of extra wisdom' and that the courts, barristers and judges 'need to be at the forefront' (B3M) of such education. Counsel noted that it was possible to recognise when defence advocates 'hit upon' a (mistaken) assumption as 'you can see a lot of … raised eyebrows' (B34M). Here then, we can see the process of affect, whereby the semiotic regime enters into the material, shifting the territory and battling to move the jury towards a different basin of attraction. Of course, which affectual force eventually wins this battle, that is succeeds in moving the jury towards an actual and finalised verdict, is a different matter and one that is prone to emergence and non-linearity.

To capitalise upon their effectiveness, it was perceived important for the judge 'to tailor them to the individual case' (B2M) and crucially, their ability to influence the jury was perceived to emanate from the fact 'they come from the judge' (B20M) and not just the prosecutor. Only a couple of advocates expressed misgivings, with one stating that 'they are wrong in principle' on the basis that they amounted to the judge 'giving evidence' (B33M), which is not their role. However, for the majority, the directions being delivered by the judge played a key function in their positive reception: 'if you asked me to defend the Act, I'll probably struggle, but if you ask me to defend what the judges say [in the form of a direction], that's a lot easier' (B28M). Certain barristers were 'thrilled' that the directions provided a mechanism via which the judge could educate jurors in a manner that was not always possible for them. Accordingly, it was considered advantageous that 'a judge is able to go a lot further than they ever were before' (B9F). These arguments reaffirm barristers' preference for developments that are perceived to emerge from and be part of the system (i.e. the Judicial College) and once again position the judiciary as a pivotal affective body within the courtroom assemblage, critically engaged in the process of sense-making.

Barristers also argued that the directions had closed down an avenue of defence questioning whereby myths would be drawn upon to discredit the complainant's account. Although this is evidently not true in many cases, as we explore below, it was argued by some to be 'pointless' to ask questions of this manner 'because the judge will say ... people don't react in the same way' (B20M). Thus, in principle, the directions amount to a budding 'line of flight' or a relative deterritorialisation which have the potential to institute a shift away from established norms and scripts and in turn, trial outcomes (although as noted, the extent to which this shift results in a guilty verdict is a different matter). However, through these moments we can better explore processes of policy implementation, the possibility of moving individuals off stable attractors and understand in further depth, the territory of the courtroom.

Discrepancy was evident in terms of the extent to which the mistaken assumptions were utilised, pointing to non-linearity in judicial approach. Some advocates noted that they were 'wheeled out all the time' (B20M) whilst for others, this was not typically the case. Temkin et al. (2018) identified that whilst certain judges adeptly addressed rape myths through the use of the directions, for others, there was an abject failure to incorporate them into their practice. Similarly, one of our barrister's commented that it was 'depressing' (B24F) that they still had to request a direction to be given and another noted that 'many judges choose not to, because a lot of judges are still very, very old school' (B8F). This again indicates the ongoing pull of basins of attraction relating to rape myths. Changing practice and patterns of behaviours is not an easy endeavour, but one that requires iterative implementation, ongoing feedback loops and adaptive management, as we come on to explore.

3.3.1 *Defence Counsel, Myths and Reterritorialisation*

Although positive perspectives on the mistaken assumptions were not limited to prosecutorial practice, when speaking about defence work, there was a greater sense of barristers being 'quite upset by the nature of some of them' (B8F). This was felt particularly strongly when the jury were warned not to surmise that inconsistencies in complainants' accounts were indicative of the allegation not being true, as it was felt that this is 'running coach and horses through most people's defence' (B17F). However, this did not mean that defending barristers were unable to 'work around' the directions. A significant minority noted that their defence tactics required espousing myths, supporting research which indicates that misconceptions continue to be kept relevant by defence (and prosecution) advocates, even though they are sometimes resisted through judicial direction and prosecutor comments (Smith and Skinner 2017; Westera et al. 2017; Zydervelt et al. 2017; Smith 2018; Temkin et al. 2018). Our participants argued that their use of myths arose from fulfilling their duty to the client (see Gunby and Carline 2019), which sometimes involved 'manipulating the juror's minds' (B35M) and 'saying things in your closing speech that will impact upon a jury' (B34M). Thus, we can see how a system tends towards certain basins of attraction and patterns of behaviour, which are difficult—albeit not impossible—to alter.

Barristers reported that the mistaken assumptions were often challenged in defence barristers' closing speeches, highlighting how advocates engage in a reterritorialisation. Whilst stereotypes were not necessarily presented as true, jurors were still asked to consider whether they were true in 'this' specific case (Smith and Skinner 2017). In mapping this reterritorialisation we can see how expression and discourse are used to move the jury, draw a plane of composition and engage in techniques of affect which link to various basins of attraction. However, counsel were not uncritical (or entirely comfortable) using such tactics, implicating a potential space for a line of flight and opportunity for a different form of practice to emerge—an argument we revisit in Chap. 4. What is of importance here is that any change and transformation in the system is perceived to be better driven by bottom-up emergence and by those who have an intensive sense of the courtroom.

3.4 Intensive Sense: Policies, Practice and Experience

The importance of developing an intensive sense of the rape courtroom was reiterated by almost every barrister and critical to discussions regarding the experience of those who were involved in creating law, CPS policy and engaged in decision-making processes. There was very real concern that the experience of those deciding whether or not a case should be charged was 'limited to the magistrate's court' and consequently these individuals 'really don't understand the dynamics of the jury trial' (B19M). Similarly, it was lamented that many decisions related to case-building, investigations and prosecutorial practice were driven by policies and a person 'in an office who's never seen anybody, who's never met anybody, [and who] are pulling the strings and you're, a bit hamstrung by what they want to do' (B31F). It was argued that while many of the policies and reforms may be well-intentioned, the difficulty was that they did not translate into courtroom practice, because 'they're not drafted by people who actually have to stand up there and speak to twelve real people about this' (B21F). It was argued that while there was a 'book' on everything, in reality, there was a 'chasm' between what was 'in that book and what I see in practice' (B13M). Again then, we see the ongoing tension between the production of top-down provisions and the daily, intensive flows of the courtroom experience.

Furthermore, a significant majority of barristers expressed unease at the increased use of solicitor advocates to defend rape cases. It was argued that these practitioners infrequently had the training or experience needed to prepare and present a case. The use of solicitor advocates was explicitly linked to cost cutting tactics, namely, the 40% cumulative decrease in spending on justice between 2010/2011 and 2019/2020 (Parliament 2017), which was considered to do a 'disservice' to defendants and complainants alike. The use of low-skilled practitioners makes little sense when reflecting on the potential to undermine the vast investment that has been made in improving policies, practices and processes related to rape and the treatment of complainants more broadly. In terms of prosecuting rape cases, it was also argued to be 'very rare' in recent years to appoint a Queen's Counsel (senior barrister) to a case, despite their complex nature. The exception, however, was in relation to high profile/celebrity cases—which are not the norm—but which were frequently being allocated senior advocates due to perceived political/PR reasons and 'to keep up the appearance' (B39F) that all rapes are dealt with similarly. The use of QCs was not, however, considered a positive step if the barrister in question had little experience of sex crime:

> I'm sure they're brilliant ... and they'd be first choice for all kinds of cases, but not for these. You want someone who's been slogging away at rape for years and years and years and just knows ... the subtleties. (B5F)

The importance of having dedicated and specialist representation in rape cases was considered crucial: 'I think you can't dabble. If you're going to do it, you've got to really do it' (B4F), on the basis that the pace of change is 'quick, in terms of the law and in terms of practice and in terms of the whole approach'. As such, it was important to be 'really selective' (B13M) regarding the allocation of practitioners. These views also point towards processes of territorialisation. More specifically, they highlight barristers' concerns regarding perceived threats to the courtroom territory and the potential clash of territories. We explore these issues further in the next chapter.

3.5 Conclusion

Throughout the data, we can see the significance barristers placed on bottom-up developments, as opposed to the imposition of top-down overcoding by legislators and policy makers. Measures could be resisted unless they corresponded with barristers' intensive sense of the problem field of the courtroom and their preference for smooth over striated space. Their views also showed how, within the rape courtroom assemblage, there is a significant intermingling of the semiotic and material regimes. Their perspectives highlight the importance they attached to having experience of the system, or to put it another way, of being an integral part of the system. This also linked to their sceptical views regarding reforms and policies produced by those who do not have an everyday working understanding of trials, or specifically, do not have an intensive sense of the rape courtroom, the problem field and phase space. In order to actively participate in the techniques of affect and draw a plane of composition, it is vital that bodies/practitioners are emerged in and interact with the system. In the absence of such, barristers perceived people to lack the ability and knowledge to actively engage in and reform the system. They do not have an intensive sense of the assemblage; of its flows, forces, affect-events, singularities and attractors, all of which are vital to the production of transformations.

References

Beres, M. (2010). Sexual Miscommunication? Untangling Assumptions About Sexual Communication Between Casual Sexual Partners. *Culture, Health and Sexuality, 12*(1), 1–14.

Carline, A., & Gunby, G. (2011). 'How an Ordinary Jury Makes Sense of It Is a Mystery': Barristers' Perspectives on Rape, Consent and the Sexual Offences Act 2003. *Liverpool Law Review, 32*(3), 237–250.

Carline, A., & Gunby, C. (2017). Rape Politics, Policies and Practice: Exploring the Tensions and Unanticipated Consequences of Well-Intended Victim-Focused Measures. *The Howard Journal, 56*, 34–52.

Carline, A., Gunby, C., & Taylor, S. (2018). Too Drunk to Consent? Exploring the Contestations and Disruptions in Male-Focused Sexual Violence Prevention Interventions. *Social and Legal Studies, 27*(3), 299–322.

Cook, K. (2011). Rape Investigation and Prosecution: Stuck in the Mud? *Journal of Sexual Aggression, 17*(3), 250–262.

Cowan, S. (2007). Freedom and Capacity to Make a Choice: A Feminist Analysis of Consent in the Criminal Law of Rape. In V. Munro & C. Stychin (Eds.), *Sexuality and the Law: Feminist Engagements* (pp. 51–71). Abingdon: Glasshouse Press Routledge-Cavendish.

Ellison, L., & Munro, V. (2013). Better the Devil You Know? 'Real Rape' Stereotypes and the Relevance of a Previous Relationship in (Mock) Juror Deliberations. *The International Journal of Evidence and Proof, 17*(4), 299–322.

Finch, E., & Munro, V. (2006). Breaking Boundaries? Sexual Consent in the Jury Room. *Legal Studies, 26*(3), 303–320.

Gunby, C., & Carline, A. (2019). The Emotional Particulars of Working on Rape Cases: Doing Dirty Work, Managing Emotional Dirt and Conceptualizing 'Tempered Indifference'. *British Journal of Criminology.* https://doi.org/10.1093/bjc/azz054.

Gunby, C., Carline, A., & Beynon, C. (2010). Alcohol Related Rape Cases: Barristers' Perspectives on the Sexual Offences Act 2003 and Its Impact on Practice. *Journal of Criminal Law, 74*(6), 579–600.

Gunby, C., Carline, A., & Beynon, C. (2012). Regretting It After? Perspectives on Alcohol Consumption, Nonconsensual Sex and False Allegations of Rape. *Social and Legal Studies, 22*(1), 87–106.

Hohl, K., & Stanko, B. (2015). Complaints of Rape and the Criminal Justice System: Fresh Evidence on the Attrition Problem in England and Wales. *European Journal of Criminology, 12*(3), 324–341.

Home Office. (2006). *The Sexual Offences Act 2003: A Stocktake.* London: Home Office.

Judicial College. (2019). *The Crown Court Compendium. Part 1: Trial Management and Summing Up.* London: Judicial College.

Larcombe, W., Fileborn, B., Powell, N., & Hanley, N. (2016). 'I Think It's Rape and I Think He Would Be Found Not Guilty': Focus Group Perceptions of (Un)Reasonable Belief in Consent in Rape Law. *Social and Legal Studies, 25*(5), 611–629.

Muehlenhard, C. L., Humphreys, T. P., Jozkowski, K. N., & Peterson, Z. D. (2016). The Complexities of Sexual Consent Among College Students: A Conceptual and Empirical Review. *The Journal of Sex Research, 53*(4–5), 457–487.

Parliament. (2017). *Ministry of Justice Expenditure: Written Question – 1125414.* Retrieved July 16, 2019, from https://www.parliament.uk/business/publications/written-questions-answers-statements/written-question/Commons/2017-11-13/112641/.

Smith, O. (2018). *Rape Trials in England and Wales: Observing Justice and Rethinking Rape Myths.* London: Palgrave Macmillan.

Smith, O., & Skinner, T. (2017). How Rape Myths Are Used and Challenged in Rape and Sexual Assault Trials. *Social and Legal Studies, 26*(4), 441–466.

Temkin, J. (2010). "And Always Keep A-Hold of Nurse, for Fear of Finding Something Worse": Challenging Rape Myths in the Courtroom. *New Criminal Law Review, 13*(4), 710–734.

Temkin, J., Gray, J. M., & Barrett, J. (2018). Different Function of Rape Myth Use in Court: Findings from a Trial Observation Study. *Feminist Criminology, 13*(2), 205–225.

Westera, N. J., Zydervelt, S., Kaladelfos, A., & Zajac, R. (2017). Sexual Assault Complainants on the Stand: A Historical Comparison of Courtroom Questioning. *Psychology, Crime and Law, 23*(1), 15–31.

Zydervelt, S., Zajac, R., Kaladelfos, A., & Westera, N. (2017). Lawyers' Strategies for Cross-Examining Rape Complainants: Have We Moved Beyond the 1950s? *British Journal of Criminology, 57*(3), 551–569.

CHAPTER 4

Courtroom Performances: Drama, but not Representational Drama

Abstract This chapter focuses on the material regime. We explore aspects of the rape courtroom assemblage which include various embodied practices and performances. Through this, we can map the significance placed on the ability of the body to affect and be affected and consider how this impacted barristers' perspectives on, and utilisation of, measures which have been brought in to improve the courtroom experience for rape victims. We also map, and make visible, various courtroom tactics and practices and see how these are influenced by key attractors and involve drawing a plane of composition and engaging in techniques of affect. Whilst affects and the material regime will be our primary focus, given the interconnected reality of the theory, this will also involve issues of territory and intensive sense.

Keywords Material regime • Territories • Techniques of affect • Rape • Special measures • Courtroom performances • Victimhood • Testimony

A. Carline et al., *Rape and the Criminal Trial*, Palgrave Socio-Legal Studies, https://doi.org/10.1007/978-3-030-38684-9_4

4.1 Introduction

In this chapter, the material regime becomes our primary focus, while at the same time recognising that it is not possible to completely disentangle the semiotic and the material. We explore aspects of the rape courtroom assemblage which include various embodied practices and performances. Through this, we can map issues related to the ability of the body to affect and be affected and consider how this impacted barristers' perspectives on, and utilisation of, various measures introduced to improve the courtroom experience for rape victims. We can map courtroom tactics and practices and see how these are influenced by key attractors and involve drawing a plane of composition and engaging in techniques of affect. Whilst affects and the material regime will be our primary focus, given the interconnected reality of the theory, we will also examine issues of territory and intensive sense. We develop this analysis by exploring the following five themes that emerged from the data: 'courtroom tactics, techniques and territories', 'embodied courtroom performances', 'marshalling affects: performing victimhood', 'changing cross-examination techniques?' and 'compelling performances: lines of flight'. Through this analysis, we can further understand the problem field and phase space of the courtroom.

4.2 Courtroom Tactics, Techniques and Territories

We can start to understand barristers' appreciation of the problem field (both actual and intensive) of the courtroom by exploring statements in the data which point to courtroom tactics. These can be categorised as attractors which inform techniques of affect and can be mapped in phase space. For example, almost all barristers reported placing significant focus on 'winning' rape cases, in contrast, for example, to achieving some sense of justice: 'Barristers are just hired guns, it depends who pays us. So, all I care about is how do I win, right' (B33M). Although many advocates within our sample did report 'caring' about an array of factors associated with cases, and in many respects, a focus on winning provides the means to minimise occupational conflict (see Gunby and Carline 2019), this attractor inevitably flows from the combative nature of the adversarial system. As such, the attractor of winning drives the operation of various techniques of affect and the plane of composition that barristers utilise in the courtroom: 'So, is the judge doing what I want; is my opponent doing what I want; is the witness doing what I want; is my client doing what I want, in order for me to win? (B33M). Thus, a trial was perceived to be about 'people management' (B38M) and perhaps unsurprisingly given their crucial role in proceedings, developing a good relationship with the jury: 'You've got to know a lot about human nature. You've got to be very good with people and you've got to be very good with jurors' (B13M).

We can further explore issues related to tactics and techniques of affect through barristers' discussions of the use of the Achieving Best Evidence (ABE) interview in the courtroom, and here, we also see reflections on territories emerge via a conflict between 'best evidence' and 'affective evidence'. Given that territories are constituted by practices as well as physical spaces, we can situate the use of ABE as a (relative) deterritorialisation. Namely, the interviewing technique adopted by the investigating officer is fundamentally different from the approach used by barristers, thus introducing into the courtroom a different form of practice. As noted in the Introduction, the ABE comprises the complainant's police interview, which is videoed and played in court as her evidence in chief and interviewers should adopt the cognitive interview to enhance the amount of information recalled (MoJ 2011). Furthermore, a different timeframe is introduced into court as the ABE is conducted shortly after the complaint has been made. This is again seen to support the production of best evidence as memory fades over time and an early account is more likely to be accurate and less incomplete (Loftus and Palmer 1974; Read and Connolly 2007; Westera et al. 2013a), as well as reduce the stress of giving live testimony in court (Hamlyn et al. 2004; Burton et al. 2006).

When discussing the ABE, a significant minority of barristers focused upon the affectual potential of such evidence. More specifically, the ABE was argued to support the prosecution's case on the basis that the complainant's physical appearance and comportment, as captured on video, could be seen to portray the truth of the matter and this would influence the jury accordingly:

> [I]t gives you the tremendous advantage of seeing Miss X as she was the morning which she reported it [and] when the jury hear why the defendant says she's making it up, you can say, you saw her that morning, had she gone to the police station for this reason, or that reason? And I think that is why ABEs are so good. (B5F)

This affective potential, as conceived by B5F, is however dependent upon a complaint being made immediately after the assault, whereas delayed reporting is common in sexual violence cases (Kelly et al. 2005; ONS 2017). As such, if the ABE is conducted sometime after the alleged attack, or if the complainant's performance does not conform to the expectations of rape victimhood, this may reduce what barristers perceive to be the affective capacity of that evidence.

Further, while the ABE has deterritorialising potential, it tends to result in a 'clash of territories' and subsequently elicit negative reactions from barristers. Indeed, over three-quarters of the sample argued that the ABE would impact negatively upon the prosecution's case. Resonating with opinions expressed in the Stern Review (2010 and see also Rowden et al. 2013), concerns related to the quality of the recording and the interviewing techniques. While there had been improvements, there nevertheless remained poor practice: 'some officers are really fantastic at it, others aren't so good' (B2M). Other concerns focused on the perceived loss of control over cases, especially in terms of instituting approaches that were perceived not to work in the courtroom. For example, it was argued that 'what … I find most lethal to my case when I'm prosecuting is the [ABE] interviews. Because I'm stuck with the questions that a police officer asked' (B21F). Concerns were expressed that the person conducting the interview 'asks the most ridiculous questions' (B19M) and that officers may fail to appreciate that the interview 'is actually supposed to be the account to be played to the jury' (B8F). It was argued that the police were not trained in advocacy nor had courtroom experience and thus, do not have an understanding of trial dynamics: 'I'm not convinced that the person who does the ABE interview knows about what happens in the trial and about getting a verdict' (B13M).

Through these discussions, we see a distinction emerge between best evidence and affective evidence. As noted, the ABE/cognitive interview (and other special measures) are concerned with producing best evidence, while barristers are concerned with what amounts to persuasive—or affective—evidence. Their conceptualisation of the latter is evidence that will produce an affect in the jury and move them, or, for prosecutors, improve the prospects of achieving a conviction. Thus, this is likely the cause of tensions, as opposed to any 'bad practice' on the part of officers:

> Their [the police] aims in getting evidence are totally different to mine in court. Mine will be much colder and much less emotional … they'll be

> trying not to upset the victim, they'll put them at ease. Whereas in fact, being blunt about it, that's not a concern I have. (B21F)

These findings resonate with research with prosecutors in New Zealand, who in the context of trials, perceived the use of officers' ABE/cognitive interviews to result in wordy interviewer instruction, an absence of chronology and the perusal of unnecessary detail (Westera et al. 2013b, 2017). As noted, this tension results in a clash over territories, with it being argued that 'the best results I've got are the ones where the complainant has come into court and I've been able to take them through their evidence, because then I can control my own case' (B21F). This argument can, once again, be linked to barristers' intensive sense of the courtroom and their desire to engage in techniques of affect. They position themselves, as opposed to police officers, as having a better understanding of the dynamics of the courtroom and how to produce affective testimony. However, at the same time, it was recognised that complete control over a witness's performance in court was impossible; moments of emergence and non-linearity are inevitable. Hence, if it was necessary to call the complainant to give her evidence in chief in court, this opened up the possibility of a performance that could usher negative results:

> I've done lots of cases where the ABEs were so horrendous that, right, I'm gonna call you live. And ... you're doing it with ... your fingers crossed behind your back because you've got no way of knowing whether they're gonna come up to proof, whether they're gonna go totally off piste, or whether they're just gonna crumble. (B9F)

Hence, taking control of the evidence still had the potential to produce unwanted results. There remains an inevitable emergence to live testimony that is not encountered with pre-recorded evidence in chief.

4.3 Embodied Courtroom Performances

In their desire to engender certain affects within the courtroom, barristers emphasised the importance of the jury being able to view the complainant's body and face. In relation to the ABE, concern was expressed that the positioning of the camera in the police station would often mean that the jury would be unable to see the complainant's face, shielding them from the 'intimate' reactions to the questions posed and 'the pain' (B29M) of them giving their account.[1] It was argued that 'you can tell so much from people's faces' (B28M) and that in particular, an inability to see the complainant's eyes would lead to the testimony being 'remote and detached' (B28M). Through these arguments we can see the importance barristers place on the material regime and the embodied performance of the complainant. Furthermore, advocates not only placed emphasis on the importance of the jury being able to see the body, but unanimously expressed the view that testimony that was delivered live in the courtroom, had a more significant affectual impact on the jury.

The numerous special measures introduced for vulnerable and intimidated witnesses, which include being examined over a live link, mean that a complainant may never have to appear physically in the courtroom. Despite this, all participants emphasised that when prosecuting, they wanted the complainant to be physically present in court for at least some of her testimony. Confirming anecdotal evidence in England and Wales and resonating with views from practitioners in other jurisdictions (Hamlyn et al. 2004; Burton et al. 2006; Council of HM Circuit Judges 2006; Payne 2009), barristers maintained that placing the complainant outside the courtroom had a negative impact upon a trial. It was argued that such measures 'dehumanise' (B10F) the victim and that you lose 'that bit of human intimacy' (B7F). It was felt that having the witness in court can 'be the most powerful evidence' (B18F) and thus, the use of remote testimony was 'a mistake for the evidential value of the Crown's case' (B17F). Concerns were expressed that complainants could come across as 'a bad actress or bad actor', which prevented the jury from connecting 'with the individual as a human being' (B30M). Consequently, the intensive ability of the complainant to affect the jury was perceived to be undermined:

> When you're looking at someone giving their evidence through a TV screen, it's two dimensional and you lose the emotion, you lose the tension ... and therefore, it may not have an impact on the jury. (B19M)

The perceived importance of a live account was also linked to (problematic) assumptions regarding the capacity of the body to tell the truth of the allegation and this being readable, and understood, by the jury:

> if you sit in the courtroom and if you watch somebody who is finding the process very difficult, you can tell very quickly listening to somebody if they're telling the truth or not. (B14F)

Reflecting the intermingling of the semiotic and material regimes, B14F also argued that 'much is lost in translation when the jury are looking at a face on a television screen', because juries are unable to 'pick up on the little nuances of body language' which are 'vital to understanding the meaning of something, as opposed to just the words that are spoken'.

Hence, it was deemed important for the victim to be physically present in court so that the jury could 'get a sense of them' (B7F). Again, barristers emphasised the importance of the embodied e/affective nature of being able to see 'the whites of their eyes' (B20M) and 'almost smell the person three or four feet away' (B38M). Being able to appreciate the size of the complainant, in comparison to the defendant, was also considered important and could get lost over the live link: '[S]ome people on screen just have a bulk about them and you can't actually see how young and vulnerable they may be, how tiny they may be in contrast to the defendant' (B18F). As such, a live and embodied performance was argued to change the affective atmosphere of the courtroom and the subsequent trial dynamics: 'having someone actually in court giving their evidence … you can feel the emotion, you can feel the atmosphere changing in court, it makes a big difference to the trial' (B14F). This, reportedly, produced transformative affects where 'the impact is just huge, I mean, hairs up on the back of your neck. You know, it's tangible' (B9F).

Remote complainants were also perceived to be placed at a disadvantage because the defendant would typically give his evidence live in court. The jury would therefore 'see him in the flesh' (B3M), whereas the complainant and her account would remain 'sterilised' (B11M). Concerns were expressed that the jury would often 'switch off' (B13M) during the use of video evidence and the physical presence of the defendant in the courtroom would then change the atmosphere and dynamic, or more specifically, 'everyone starts to wake up' (B13M) when he enters the witness stand. In contrast to a remote complainant, it was argued that the defendant would have the advantage of seeing how the jury reacted to his evidence and would be able to alter his presentation in response. Emphasising the importance of the courtroom performance, and how this may strengthen or weaken the affectual relationships between different bodies, it was noted that 'a disastrous sign for the prosecution … is if [the defendant] makes [the jury] laugh' (B5F). While it may be unlikely that a complainant would/could engender a similar response, she may 'get some reaction out of [the jury]' (B5F) but due to her physical absence, would remain unaware of how she was being 'read'. Hence, not being in physical proximity with the jury was held to block the intensive flow by which affects were emitted, sensed and transformations amongst bodies in the courtroom occurred.

Overall, it was argued that having the complainant live in the courtroom makes a difference between 'getting a conviction or not' (B8F). However, as we have noted, conviction rates have remained relatively stable over the last ten years, which suggests that the link between convictions and remote testimony is not as linear as counsel perceive. Empirical research suggests that the mode of delivery does not impact upon trial outcome, but rather, other (predominately extra-legal) factors do (Ellison and Munro 2013).[2] Nevertheless, barristers' sense of the impact of special measures fundamentally influenced their practice (see Carline et al. in press for a discussion). This preference for the complainant to physically appear in court led to a situation whereby experienced prosecutors would try to 'disapply special measures' (B9F), or at least, encourage complaints 'to give evidence in court from behind a screen' (B19M). Whilst 'to say that I'll persuade them to [physically] come into court is probably putting it too highly' (B11M), other barristers were more willing to 'twist witnesses' arms' (B5F) to give their evidence live.

However, conflict arose here because barristers simultaneously recognised the positive impact of special measures, especially those which ensure that the complainant does not need to enter the courtroom. Thus, we see a bifurcation point emerge that advocates must manage and which we can also situate as a potential line of flight. A key objective of special measures is to reduce stress and upset and all barristers supported this aim. In line with official rationale and research (Davies 1999; Ellison and Munro 2014), it was argued that special measures encourage reporting and continued engagement in the system. They were therefore deemed 'another tool in your armoury' (B24F) for dealing with reluctant complainants, and made the 'experience far less distressing' (B28M). Thus, advocates recognised that delivering testimony in court was an intensive experience which could produce negative affects in the complainant which needed to be stemmed: 'nobody should take a kicking for being brave enough to make an allegation' (B22M). However, barristers struggled to reconcile this tension: 'If you make it easy for people to give evidence, easier, through this sort of technology, you lose the impact of their giving evidence in court and it results in more acquittals' (B33M). It is important here to reiterate the combative nature of advocates' questioning, particularly during cross-examination, and parallel use of stereotypical rape victim scripts, and the impact these have on complainants. (Westera et al. 2017; Zydervelt et al. 2017). Thus, special measures, which focus on the location of delivering testimony, do little to protect a witness from being/feeling attacked by the defence barrister, be that via video link or otherwise. Combative practices inevitably have a negative affect on the complainant, undermine the influence of any special measure and diminish the capabilities of that victim accordingly.

In light of these debates, we can situate presence within the courtroom as a key attractor. Proximity with the complainant's fleshy body was perceived vital to producing and overcoming affects and intensive forces which would ultimately move the jury from an intensive superposition (simultaneously guilty/not guilty; victim/not victim) to an actual delivered verdict. At the same time, a line of flight emerged regarding the positive aspects of special measures, resulting in continual processes of de- and reterritorialisation.

4.4 Marshalling Affects: Performing Victimhood

As we have outlined in Chap. 2, a common theme/attractor in the courtroom assemblage is that rape cases are premised on one person's word against another. This places crucial emphasis on the testimony of the parties involved, particularly the complainant. Linking with the discussion above, the importance of the delivery of that testimony was situated as key, again pointing to the merging of the symbolic and material regimes and the relevance of embodied expression—the way things are said, and what a body does in the delivery of testimony, was viewed as having an affect. Namely, affective discourse was seen to be synonymous with embodied discourse. Barristers argued: 'You've got a word on word case. So how a victim delivers that evidence, you know, their demeanour, their face [is critical]' (B24F). B1M stated that a 'very good' performance required the complainant to give a 'good account of things'. There are, however, questions to be raised as to what amounts to a 'good account' and whether this simply means testimony that in a barrister's eyes makes 'intensive sense', that is, which can produce visceral responses in others. At the same time, barristers tended to prefer testimony that provided a coherent and linear overview of events, despite this conflicting with research on how people recount a traumatic incident. Such recollections are often non-linear, incomplete, interrupted and fragmented (Brewin 2011. See, however, Engelhard et al. 2019 for an alternative perspective). Hence, we can map a tension also highlighted in the previous chapter between intensive sense and common sense. While a coherent and linear account may seem, on some level, to make common sense, this does not necessarily mean that it will have an affective capacity, or, more specifically, carry intensive sense and the ability to move the jury.

Every barrister in our sample understood that affects needed to be managed and sensations brought into being. However, their understanding of what would affect the jury frequently intertwined with problematic discourses surrounding 'real rape' and how a 'real' victim would react in the circumstances. This, again, evidences a tension between intensive and common sense, as well as demonstrating that myths continue to operate as basins of attraction within the system. Indeed, myths were also reported to be embodied in victims' testimonies, who used them to rationalise behaviour and attribute self-blame (see Jordan 2004; Saunders 2012)—further territorialising (or fixing into place) stereotypical rape perspectives:

> And those … the stereotypes that are applied by juries are also applied by victims to themselves … you get someone coming along who's almost apologising and pointing out the errors of their conduct; I know I shouldn't have gone with him; I know I shouldn't have drunk so much. (B12F)

Myths related to attire were still seen to influence a jury: 'they're [the jury] still gonna go, the slut was wearing a skimpy top, do you know what I mean? … they still have that visceral response' (B31F). Describing the jury's reaction as 'visceral' situates it as an intensive, autonomic, embodied reaction, with advocates pinpointing and marshalling the affects that flowed from the bodily actions, fluids and emissions associated with rape, in order to maximise a complainant's account:

> I always like to ask questions like, so what was it like when you kissed the girl who'd just vomited everywhere, you know, was it nice kissing her, tasting of vomit? Um, which is normally a question that a jury think, oh, you are disgusting. (B9F)

Extreme bodily reactions on the witness stand were also recognised to have an intensive, transformative impact, which could move a jury to convict:

> Um, and when she was describing the sensation of giving oral sex to her father, and then started vomiting in the witness box, I mean, at that point I could have just sat down, and that was it, you know, he was always gonna get [convicted] after that. (B20M)

While these reactions have intensive sense in that they are recognised to provoke a response in the jury, they perpetuate misconceptions regarding the reactions of rape victims in court. Indeed, such strong responses are rare and not a standard to be strived towards.

As is clear, barristers expected victims to be traumatised in a particular way by rape and for that trauma to be emotionally visible during the trial: 'This witness was … most compelling because she came in and at the point at which I was saying to her, right, then what happened, you know, she … just went to pieces' (B20M). These views often interlinked with the discussion in the preceding section, as barristers emphasised the importance of have the victim in court, 'crying her eyes out, [as] a real person' (B6F). Similar views were expressed by those who defended, arguing that the breakdown would confirm the truth of the allegation: 'If you're defending, you don't want the jury to see anybody breaking down and crying, looking at your client, because it just reinforces the truth of the account' (B14F). However, what is key here is the emotional valence of the courtroom performance, whether that is delivered in person or remotely. Furthermore, in order to be compelling testimony had to come across as authentic and 'genuine' (B1M), otherwise it could lose its intensive quality and 'positively put jurors off' (B1M). Such expectations require complainants to carefully and strategically engage in techniques of affect, which can produce heartfelt emotion, but at the right intensity and tempo, which arguably places an unrealistic expectation onto a courtroom performance. Again, we can map a tension between what is perceived to be common sense and intensive sense, as discourses and normative scripts pervade barristers' views of what amounts to a compelling and transformative courtroom presentation—with the latter being centrally linked to a resolute focus on 'winning' a case. Indeed, the requirement to express distress, in the pursuit of securing a conviction, could lead to a detached, unsympathetic framing of the experience of the complainant:

> I don't care if she's upset, I want her to be upset, because if you've been raped, you'd be upset. For the jury to invest trust in her, she has to convey the emotion of someone who's been through that [rape] experience. (B33M)

Comments like this, which were rare, reflected what was perceived to be the type of victim response necessary to win a case, as opposed to inevitably being reflective of the advocate's personal view on rape complainants. Thus, the production of affects in order to achieve convictions was often given priority over the wellbeing of the victim. As noted, such views assume that there *is* a right way to react emotionally to rape and that such reactions can be performed within the setting of the courtroom. These perspectives conflict with the mistaken assumption directions already discussed, one of which states that complainants will display a range of emotions, including non-emotion, during the trial process (Judicial College 2019).

4.5 Changing Cross-Examination Techniques?

Reflections upon courtroom techniques and territory pertained not only to the use of special measures and victim performances, but also to recent developments relating to cross-examination approaches. Certain barristers were of the view that cross-examination was 'becoming far more restricted' (B28M) and a minority argued that this ensured 'there are rules to play by' (B7F) and was a necessary step to prevent 'ruthless' defence counsel trying 'anything' (B7F) to win their case. Thus, we can trace patterns of behaviour here but also see the early development of a possible line of flight away from established courtroom tactics. Whilst various 'restrictions' on cross-examination were undoubtedly contested, still in their infancy and relative, they nevertheless provide a potential for a radically different approach to emerge. Change in tactics was mapped onto various developments relating to the examination of vulnerable witnesses and guidance developed by the Advocates' Gateway (The Advocates Gateway n.d.), as well as a broader change in legal practice culture. Concerning the former, the Advocates Gateway is a resource providing evidence-based guidance to advocates on vulnerable witnesses and defendants. A range of toolkits now exist around the case management and questioning of those deemed vulnerable, for example, individuals with memory, sensory, communication and learning impairments, mental disorders or those of child/youth status. Having experienced a sexual offence does not make a witness immediately vulnerable, even though they are considered to be intimidated (see toolkit 10, The Advocates Gateway 2017).

For a majority, these toolkits and 'accommodations' caused tensions and were met with a level of resistance due to the perception that they restricted, limited and constrained the barrister's opportunity to develop a case. Or, put differently, impinged on their courtroom territory: 'It's a running joke that you can no longer put your case … because the list of questions is pre-checked, effectively, by a judge before you do the hearing'

(B20M). For some, these restrictions were considered 'completely unnecessary' (B23M) and to have 'almost swung' (B20M) things in favour of complainants. In a climate whereby the most vulnerable have long been marginalised from accessing justice, it is questionable how far such provisions can be constructed as 'unnecessary'. However, other barristers (including those who also raised concerns) noted that, in principle, the idea of affording protections to the most vulnerable was 'wonderful' (B22M) and met the requirements of the Convention of the Rights of Persons with Disabilities (CRPD) to access justice and permit suitable accommodations to do so.

The restrictions on cross-examination and perceived inability to 'put one's case' (B31F) when representing vulnerable clients, was argued to be unfair on defendants who were not being given a suitably comprehensive opportunity to cross-examine the witness. It was also argued that the defendant's account continued to be challenged during cross-examination whilst the vulnerable complainant's was not. However, this approach was simultaneously perceived to disadvantage the victim. Around half of the sample argued that as a consequence of not being able to fully put one's case to the complainant, elements of her account were not being fully tested. In turn, she was not being given the opportunity to provide an 'explanation for inconsistencies' (B29M). It was felt that this left the jury suspicious, asking 'what impression must that make' (B28M). In this respect, provisions designed to support vulnerable complainants were seen to be disadvantageous because 'she's protected from being asked the questions, but the ultimate aim of having her there, which is to get the conviction, is just massively undermined' (B29M). Whilst advocates' perspectives here are inevitably influenced by the threat imposed onto their territory, the impression firmly given was that these provisions could have non-linear effects in practice (see Carline and Gunby 2017). In terms of instituting intensive affects and sensations, it was also argued that by not being allowed to cross-examine on certain questions 'a lot of the impact' (B31F) of the cross-examination was lost, because you don't get 'the witness reactions' which could convince the jury that 'this man is guilty' (B11M). In contrast, it was considered 'absolutely fabulous' from a defence perspective 'not to actually have to challenge somebody who will then very obviously and very genuinely get upset' (B21F).

In addition to these more official developments, barristers stated that there had been more organic changes in cross-examination practice. It was argued by a minority that a robust cross-examination could be achieved without 'shouting and screaming' (B26F) and telling a complainant 'you're lying' (B27F) but instead, through 'a very positive assertion in a way the jury and the witness will understand' (B26F). Whilst it was recognised that cross-examination will still be difficult, it was argued that it can be 'done professionally' (B37F) and that there should not be scope for 'bullying, barracking and making people cry (B20M)'. This line of flight away from historic standards can, however, be traced back to concerns regarding the impact of 'barracking' upon the jury. Two barristers explicitly commented that adopting an aggressive questioning style would only serve to 'alienate the jury' (B10F) and in light of needing to 'make friends' with them, you 'don't slag off the complainant' (B1M). Along these lines, B12F argued: 'I'm never particularly rude to victims because I've never found it helpful, in terms of a jury; they don't like someone having a go.' In parallel, and as noted in Chap. 2, a personal and reflexive perspective on defence work emerged, which again can be mapped as a potential bifurcation point and budding line of flight away from problematic questioning techniques. B27F, for example, commented:

> there's this horrible feeling before you start cross-examining a rape complainant, I don't want to reduce them to tears, I don't want to destroy their lives, I don't want to make them re-live what they've been through. I want to make it as easy experience as possible in court.

B35M also noted that they 'felt bad' about the adoption of 'forensic techniques' which were devised to highlight inconsistencies within testimony. This conflict could lead to the adoption of neutralising techniques (Ashforth et al. 2007; Gunby and Carline 2019), in order to distance oneself from aspects of their practice and render manageable intense and diminishing sensations:

> And, um, I think I personally just try not to think about it too much. So, I treat it in a very academic way, you know, this is … reading this, applying the facts to the law. … And then really just try and leave it behind. (B8F)

While research indicates that defence practices can still be re-victimising and excessive (Westera et al. 2017; Zydervelt et al. 2017), these views indicate that certain barristers are reflective upon their practice. The importance for our work is the existence of a bifurcation point and potential line of flight that can be explored by policy makers to institute alternative practice. We can map a move, or at least some desire to move away from traditional aggressive approaches, to those which are potentially more ethical in nature. Thus, a space to explore more flourishing approaches to cross-examination may be possible.

4.6 Compelling Performances: Lines of Flight

In this final section, we explore barristers' accounts of unexpected courtroom performances which were deemed to be compelling, but which can be seen to challenge dominant expectations and stereotypes of victimhood. For example, performances which were more spontaneous, affirming and transgressive and in which the complainant displayed agency and assertiveness, thus countering previously explored expectations of the 'ideal', emotional victim. B9F recalled a case in which the complainant, while delivering her testimony in court, engaged in a disruptive expression that was seen to have a lasting and transformative affect (and effect) upon the jury:

> that moment where … the witness looks past you when you're asking them questions and they just go, I just want him to know I've never forgotten. And it's dynamite. You can't pay for stuff like that. As a prosecutor it's absolutely amazing.

Thus, we can map a line of flight and a deterritorialisation away from traditional, highly vulnerable rape victim testimony. We can also see the potential for self-organisation and the emergence of an unexpected performance in the courtroom that can have an intensive impact.

Similar eruptive/affective moments were identified by B29M and B33M, both involving in-court performances where the complainant confronted the defendant. With the latter, the barrister noted that the complainant had expressed her wish to 'face' the defendant and 'see him' in court and whilst giving her evidence 'shouted the word pervert'. Such an outburst can be understood as the expression of sensation in language and an emergent moment whereby the intensive relationship between the complainant and accused is rendered perceptible to the jury. In so doing, the jury connects with the gut-wrenching desperation and authenticity of the outburst. B29M's case involved a complainant initially being cross-examined in court with the use of screens, eventually asking for them to be removed. The barrister continued:

> Over the course of the afternoon, she got more and more confident 'til she was looking past me—I was putting something to her—she was looking past me and, um, pointing at him and saying, that's wrong and you know that's wrong, you dirty bastard.

In such moments, we can view the complainant as being involved in drawing a plane of composition, one which may occur quite unexpectedly, and again see emergence and self-organisation within the courtroom assemblage. These intensive moments were not, however, limited to in-court performances but could also occur over the live link, indicating that it is possible to engage in techniques of affect remotely:

> And she gave evidence alright on the video link. But the best thing she did was, she shouted to—it was her uncle who'd raped her as a child—and she shouted 'I can't see you but if you can see or you can hear me, you know what you did to me'. (B33M)

Compelling performances were not limited to those which involved a sudden outburst but could include more prescriptive accounts. The key dimension was that testimony had to make (intensive) sense and resonate with the audience. B24F noted that the 'most impressive victims' were the ones who gave 'quite a personal account … from the witness box'. It was also noted that compelling performances could emerge from those who had been 'properly supported' pre-trial, as they were better able to 'stand up properly to the questions that they're asked' (B12F). At the same time, it must be recognised that the embodiment of the confidence, literacy and language skill necessary to present as compelling will not be accessible to all. It is therefore important not to present these as expected or ideal performances, but rather recognise them as an unusual and novel emergence within the system.

The lines of flight emerging from the data also relate to circumstances pertaining to the rape, with barristers acknowledging that the system can and does accommodate victims who have been drinking, who knew their perpetrator, who lacked injuries and who went back to the accused's home. For example, B34M recounted a case in which the complainant was 'phenomenally compelling' on the ABE 'because she says, oh, I drank far too much, I never normally do that … you know, I really shouldn't have'. Linking this with the above quote from B24F, the compellability seems to emerge from the frankness of the account, giving it its intensive affect. At the same time, however, we can see processes of reterritorialisation, as the complainant engages in self-criticism—'I really shouldn't have'—which arguably captures the line of flight and brings it back to the normative ideal victim type.[3] A further example, which does not appear to be captured by reterritorialising tendencies, was presented by B31F:

> that was an unusual one ... her behaviour that night was so promiscuous that you would have expected the jury to go, don't like that at all. But she was so unapologetically promiscuous, she literally stood in the witness box and went, yeah. ... I sleep with everybody that I want to sleep with, and I quite enjoy sex ... and I don't see a problem with that. And they [the jury] kind of went, alright, fair enough.

As Larcombe (2002) has argued, this does not mean that the ideal victim script does not have currency but rather, those women who get convictions in their cases are often the ones who establish credibility through acts of subversion and resistance in court. That is, women who will not 'withdraw from engagement, they will not refuse to answer questions, they will not acquiesce, relent or give in' (Larcombe 2002: 142). Thus, if a survivor can endure the process of cross-examination, she can be afforded the opportunity to present as victimised, but as persuasive, credible and resistant—both now and at the time of the rape. Whilst Larcombe acknowledges that the ability to offer such an account is tied to age, ethnicity, language skill and class, if resistance is possible, it offers the potential to reconceptualise the successful rape complainant as someone with a strong sense of self/her experience, rather than being someone who is at all times virtuous.

4.7 Conclusion

Through this analysis, it has been possible to render perceptible the emphasis barristers placed upon the affectual capacity of the complainant's body and the importance of moving and transforming the jury. These perspectives underpinned advocates' views on and receptivity towards using special measures, particularly those which placed the complainant outside of the courtroom. They also informed their conceptualisation of what amounted to a transformative and/or compelling courtroom performance and their engagement with techniques of affect. This, however, should not be read as suggesting that we support abolishing special measures. They play an important role in protecting complainants from certain negative affects at trial, which barristers themselves recognised. Whilst perhaps different in nature to their in-person counterparts, we identify that intensive affects can also flow from remote testimony. Thus, the question to explore with practitioners is how, via technology, the forces of affects can be most productively marshalled to bring about the desired sensations and transformations.

Participants' conceptualisations of transformative and affective performances could also be seen to be frequently influenced by 'real rape' discourses. At the same time, lines of flight emerged and presentations that did not adhere to victimhood could be deemed credible. Again, we argue that such lines of flight should be explored and capitalised upon in future policy efforts aimed at dislodging dominant, normative courtroom scripts.

Notes

1. For a detailed analysis of the use and issues with remote testimony/courtroom participation in Australia, and suggestions for reform, see Rowden et al. 2013.
2. However, as Ellison and Munro (2013) note, a limitation of their research is that the complainant delivered the testimony with the same emotional state, regardless of the mode of delivery, and it is the emotional salience of the testimony that barristers perceive to have affectual force.
3. However, we recognise that it is not possible to deduce from the data whether the ability and willingness to self-sensor in this way played a role in her testimony coming to constitute compelling.

References

Advocates Gateway. (2017). Identifying Vulnerability in Witnesses and Parties and Making Adjustments. *Toolkit 10.* Retrieved from https://www.theadvocatesgateway.org/images/toolkits/10-identifying-vulnerability-in-witnesses-and-parties-and-making-adjustments-2017.pdf.

Advocates Gateway. (n.d.). *Toolkits.* Retrieved October 10, 2018, from https://www.theadvocatesgateway.org/toolkits.

Ashforth, B. E., Kreiner, G. E., Clark, M. A., & Fugate, M. (2007). Normalizing Dirty Work: Managerial Tactics for Countering Occupational Taint. *Academy of Management Journal, 50*, 149–174.

Brewin, C. R. (2011). The Nature and Significance of Memory Disturbance in Posttraumatic Stress Disorder. *Annual Review of Clinical Psychology, 7*, 203–227.

Burton, M., Evans, R., & Sanders, A. (2006). *Are Special Measures for Vulnerable and Intimidated Witnesses Working? Evidence from the Criminal Justice Agencies.* Home Office Online Report 01/06.

Carline, A., & Gunby, C. (2017). Rape Politics, Policies and Practice: Exploring the Tensions and Unanticipated Consequences of Well-Intended Victim-Focused Measures. *The Howard Journal of Crime and Justice, 56*(1), 34–52.

Carline, A., Gunby, C., & Murray, J. (in press). "And That's Why Street-Wise Complainants Now Always Give Evidence Behind Screens, Live": Exploring the Intensive Affects of the Courtroom. In K. Duncanson & E. Henderson (Eds.), *Courthouse Design and Social Justice.* Abingdon: Routledge.

Council of HM Council Judges. (2006). *Convicting Rapists and Protecting Victims: A Consultation Response of the Council of Her Majesty's Circuit Judges.* London: Council of HM Circuit Judges

Davies, G. (1999). The Impact of Television on the Presentation and Reception of Children's Testimony. *International Journal of Law and Psychiatry, 22*(3–4), 241–256.

Ellison, L., & Munro, V. (2013). Better the Devil You Know? 'Real Rape' Stereotypes and the Relevance of a Previous Relationship in (Mock) Juror Deliberations. *The International Journal of Evidence and Proof, 17*(4), 299–322.

Ellison, L., & Munro, V. (2014). A "Special" Delivery? Exploring the Impact of Screens, Live-Links and Video Recorded Evidence on Mock Juror Deliberation in Rape Trials. *Social & Legal Studies, 23*(1), 3–29.

Engelhard, I. M., McNally, R. J., & van Schie, K. (2019). Retrieving and Modifying Traumatic Memories: Recent Research Relevant to Three Controversies. *Current Direction in Psychological Science, 28*(1), 91–96.

Gunby, C., & Carline, A. (2019). The Emotional Particulars of Working on Rape Cases: Doing Dirty Work, Managing Emotional Dirt and Conceptualizing 'Tempered Indifference'. *British Journal of Criminology.* https://doi.org/10.1093/bjc/azz054.

Hamlyn, B., Phelps, A., Turtle, J., & Sattar, G. (2004). *Are Special Measures Working? Evidence from Surveys of Vulnerable and Intimidated Witnesses.* Home Office Research Study 283. London: Home Office.

Jordan, J. (2004). Beyond Belief?: Police, Rape and Women's Credibility. *Criminology and Criminal Justice, 4*(1), 29–59.

Judicial College. (2019). *The Crown Court Compendium. Part 1: Trial Management and Summing Up.* London: Judicial College.

Kelly, L., Lovett, J., & Regan, L. (2005). *A Gap or a Chasm? Attrition in Reported Rape Cases.* Home Office Research Study 293, Home Office Research, Development and Statistics Directorate. London: Home Office.

Larcombe, W. (2002). The 'Ideal' Victim v Successful Rape Complainants: Not What You Might Expect. *Feminist Legal Studies, 10*(2), 131–148.

Loftus, E. F., & Palmer, J. C. (1974). Reconstruction of Automobile Destruction: An Example of the Interaction Between Language and Memory. *Journal of Verbal Learning and Verbal Behavior, 13*, 585–589.

Ministry of Justice (MoJ). (2011). *Achieving Best Evidence in Criminal Proceedings Guidance on Interviewing Victims and Witnesses, and Guidance on Using Special Measures*. London: Ministry of Justice.

Office for National Statistics (ONS). (2017). *Overview of Violent Crime and Sexual Offences*. Retrieved from https://www.ons.gov.uk/peoplepopulationandcommunity/crimeandjustice/compendium/focusonviolentcrimeandsexualoffences/yearendingmarch2016/overviewofviolentcrimeandsexualoffences.

Payne, S. (2009). *Redefining Justice: Addressing the Individual Needs of Victims and Witnesses*. London: Home Office.

Read, J. D., & Connolly, A. (2007). The Effects of Delay on Long-Term Memory for Witnessed Events. In M. P. Toglia, J. D. Read, D. R. Ross, & R. C. L. Lindsay (Eds.), *Handbook of Eyewitness Psychology: Volume I. Memory for Events* (pp. 117–155). New York: Lawrence Erlbaum Associates.

Rowden, E., Wallace, A., Tait, D., Hanson, M., & Jones, D. (2013). *Gateways to Justice: Design and Operational Guidelines for Remote Participation in Court Proceedings*. Sydney: University of Western Sydney. Retrieved from http://www.uws.edu.au/justice/justice/publications.

Saunders, C. (2012). The Truth, the Half-Truth, and Nothing Like the Truth: Reconceptualizing False Allegations of Rape. *The British Journal of Criminology, 52*(6), 1152–1171.

Stern Review. (2010). *A Report by Baroness Vivien Stern CBE of an Independent Review into How Rape Complaints Are Handled by Public Authorities in England and Wales*. London: Home Office.

Westera, N. J., Kebbell, M. R., & Milne, B. (2013a). Losing Two Thirds of the Story: A Comparison of the Video-Recorded Police Interview and Live Evidence of Rape Complainants. *Criminal Law Review, 4*, 290–308.

Westera, N. J., Kebbell, M. R., & Milne, B. (2013b). It Is Better, but Does It Look Better? Prosecutor Perspectives of Using Rape Complainant Interviews as Evidence. *Psychology, Crime and Law, 19*(7), 595–610.

Westera, N. J., Zydervelt, S., Kaladelfos, A., & Zajac, R. (2017). Sexual Assault Complainants on the Stand: A Historical Comparison of Courtroom Questioning. *Psychology, Crime and Law, 23*(1), 15–31.

Zydervelt, S., Zajac, R., Kaladelfos, A., & Westera, N. (2017). Lawyers' Strategies for Cross-Examining Rape Complainants: Have We Moved Beyond the 1950s? *British Journal of Criminology, 57*(3), 551–569.

CHAPTER 5

Deleuze's Materialist Philosophy of Affect and Sense

Abstract This chapter extends the understanding of our approach by setting out a more detailed and philosophically advanced exploration of the theoretical framework, aimed at those already familiar with the theory. The theoretical framework of the intensive ontological register is fully explored, together with the intensive incorporeals that operate within that register. These include sensation, bodies, affects and affective atmospheres, together with complex composites of intensities in Deleuze's logic of sense and the conceptualisation of planes of organisation and composition. This chapter, further, explores and establishes the philosophical background of the book's pervasive theoretical methodology of intensive problem space and the workings of intensive problematics.

Keywords Intensive ontological regime • Incorporeals • Affects • Sensation • Sense • Plane of composition • Phase space

5.1 Introduction

This chapter and the next provide a full account of the new materialist synthetic theoretical framework adopted in this book and explore in depth and detail some of the key concepts we have already introduced and deployed. The adopted framework is that of Deleuze and Guattari's

A. Carline et al., *Rape and the Criminal Trial*, Palgrave Socio-Legal Studies, https://doi.org/10.1007/978-3-030-38684-9_5

affective assemblage theory, supported by the underlying Deleuzian materialist philosophy of affect and sense, and recent new understandings of systemic self-organisation and emergence from complexity science and theory. We explore Deleuze's materialist philosophy of affect and sense that has driven much of the affective turn in contemporary theory. The theoretical framework of the intensive ontological register is fully explored, together with the intensive incorporeals that operate in the intensive ontological register. These include sensation, bodies, affects and affective atmospheres, together with complex composites of intensities in Deleuze's logic of sense and the conceptualisation of planes of organisation and composition. This chapter, further, explores and establishes the philosophical background of the book's pervasive theoretical methodology of intensive problem space and the workings of intensive problematics.

5.2 Deleuze's Materialist Philosophy of the Social Field

Deleuze's materialist philosophy of affect and sense, in common with the broader field of new materialism and the affective turn, develops a philosophy of the primacy of processes and with ontology theorised as ontogenesis and with the direct felt reality of what is known as intensive relations (Deleuze 1988a, 1990, 1991, 1992, 1994, 2006. See also Massumi 1992; Alliez 2004; Grosz 2017). It is a philosophy of immanent forces that create and control the world. Deleuze's ontological immanence assumes no transcendence, no theological creator, no morality, no eminence and no organisation by formed ideals, external models or pre-given forms. Rather, immanence is conceptualised as ontological genesis as dynamic relations not of form and matter, but of materials and forces and the movement of matter (Deleuze 2006: 23). Thus, the Platonist world of essences and universals and formed things is replaced by events and affects as jets of singularities, and a world of Being is replaced by a world of becoming (Deleuze 1990: 56).

This exploration involves conceptualising the social field, and in turn the focus of social inquiry, as comprising, exploring and understanding the relationship between two different ontological registers of the intensive and the actual. This involves an appreciation that the intensive social field is *generative and coincident* to the more familiar more actual social field. Significantly, the theorisation of the distinction and relationship between the intensive and the actual draws out the difference in conceptual and methodological frameworks and the tools adequate to thinking and operating these two different registers. This enables a new understanding and knowledge of the social field in terms of intensive processes of becoming, expression, sensation, intensive bodies, affects, events, sense and continuous social transformation. It further enables an understanding of the plane of composition, and its relation to the plane of organisation, and an understanding of Deleuze's logic of sense and its relationship to the logic of representation. This includes how the logic of sense operates on the plane of composition, how the logic of representation operates on the plane of organisation and how representation on the plane of organisation tends to obscure and neutralise the dynamics of the plane of composition.

5.3 Deleuze's Materialism: The Actual and Intensive; Corporeals and Incorporeals

The fundamental feature of Deleuze's materialist philosophy is the positing of an intensive ontological register alongside and conditioning the actualised ontological order, and of incorporeals operating alongside and conditioning corporeals. In order to think through the emergent self-organisation and the movement of matter there must be an incorporeal dimension in which the becomings of matter and bodies occur, and in which matter and bodies undergoing change or becoming other can be conceptualised (Grosz 2017: 87). The juxtaposition of incorporeal with materialism may at first appear contradictory, but as Grosz has made clear: '[e]very materialism requires a frame, a non-material localisation, a becoming space and time that cannot exist in the same way with the same form as the objects of things that they frame' (2017: 28). Hence, there are necessarily incorporeal forces that we must assume for our material organisation. These are immaterial forces that condition powers of movement and determinate relations of motion and rest; they are the incorporeal conditions for the possible and actual existence of matter and bodies and the subsisting condition of material existence (Grosz 2017: 28).

As such, the intensive world incorporates an immanent relationality that is real but not actual. In incorporeal materialism, matter is not adequately defined by extension (what is actual and corporeal). Rather, what is real must be understood as encompassing both the material and the immaterial. Nevertheless, in this body in motion, incorporeal events are distinct from the actual actions and passions of the body and distinct from extensive states of affairs and emotion. On one side there is an incorporeal non-representational idea and on the other the material body. This intensive register is, however, coincident with the actual register. Indeed, in Deleuze's ontology the world is a process of ontogenesis in which the intensive incorporeal register is generative of the actual corporeal world. Described in another way, the actual world is the arrest and termination of the ontogenesis of the intensive world.[1]

From the perspective of the embodied materiality of social fields—for example, the embodied materiality of a criminal courtroom—this necessary intensive incorporeal dimension of corporeality is an excess that subsists and inheres in materiality as continuous change and in intensive events, affects and intensive sense. This excessive intensive dimension is lived in sensation and affect. A body or situation may be more or less submerged in an intensive field, or transition, from an actual social field into an intensive social field or vice versa. However, the two social regimes are always coincident, there side by side, intermingling and moving within one another. The intensive field is a force field of the yet to be established, what will become forces of the intensive field of different speeds and slownesses, forces that enter into each other, some forces overpowering other forces, forces move through the intensive field.

Hence, in this materialism there is a necessary doubling of a material and corporeal actual world with an immaterial and incorporeal world, which is conceptualised as the intensive world. Accordingly, the intensive social field can be explained as that which comprises the incorporeal intensities of sensation, bodies, affects, atmospheres, sensation and sense and the plane of composition, together with a conceptual framework of a problem field which is composed of continuous and discontinuous multiplicities. Within this framework, incorporeals assume significance as they are 'the capacities of material bodies or material somethings to become more or other than what they are, the conditions of their complexity' (Grosz 2017: 31). Hence, they are immaterial forces that must be assumed for material organisation (Grosz 2017: 124), the conditions for complexity and that which orientates and organises material self-organisation and emergence. Incorporeals are what enables a body to be conceptualised as undergoing change or becoming other. Hence, they provide the conditions that uphold, enable and complicate materialism. They produce the conditions for change, becomings—bodies/matter becoming more than what they are—and conditions that enable the conceptualisation of the process as undergoing change or becoming other (Grosz 2017: 31).

5.4 Exploring the Intensive Register Further

We can now begin to explore the intensive register in a little further detail. As noted, the intensive ontogenetic register is the necessarily coincident and generative incorporeal doubling of the actually existent register of the world. This ontological register is intensive because ontogenetically, pre-actualised intensities have not been cancelled out. Rather, all is disequilibrium, drawing a corporeal-incorporeal line of the becoming of the world. It can be understood as an ontogenetic register of becoming and intensive transformation in 'processes of encounters that change bodies and that enable them to undergo new affects and new encounters' (Grosz 2017: 62). The logic of this intensive organisation is completely asymmetrical to the logic of extensive actualised organisation, but nevertheless it is a rigorous, understandable and steerable logic. This is a logic of sensation and sense and simultaneously 'sense laden excesses of materiality' (Deleuze 1990, 2006), of the intensive exchanges and events of intensive bodies in sense and affect.

Understanding the intensive social field is crucial to the entire project of reconceptualising the courtroom as an affective assemblage theory. It is the field of immaterial and material bodies and affects in movement and an embodied and emplaced materiality. It is a field of intensities that are unconscious, extra-propositional, sub-representational, impersonal, pre-individuated singularities and in process intensive individuations and of forces of 'unformed matters and nonformal functions' (Deleuze 2006: 64). The field is in perpetual disequilibrium, with complex social forces placed against other complex social forces in differential relations that do not cancel out in intensity (Deleuze 1988b: 63). We can further understand the intensive as comprising an imperceptible, yet unimposed constitutive field of cohesion, that enable bodies and objects to come into being and come to mean something, without these transformations being in anyway corporeal themselves (Grosz 2017: 32).

Significantly, in the intensive social field 'things are surrounded and suffused by incorporeals, which enable them to have extension or occupy a location (place), to have a time or history (time), exert affects beyond themselves' (Grosz 2017: 38). The intensive social field is both the incorporeal networks of forces that compose and connect, and the realised material networks of forces that cause and connect. The intensive social field is thus the processes of subjective, social, ethical and political becomings and emergence. In so becoming, the intensive social field changes the operation and meaning of power, with power 'no longer fundamentally normative, like it was in its disciplinary forms, it's affective' (Massumi 2013: 30). Rather, the intensive social field opens up potentially new relationships and new type of thought irreducible to knowledge (Deleuze 1988b: 62).

5.4.1 *Understanding the Intensive Movement of Matter and Becomings*

Key to understanding the importance of intensive incorporeality and the self-emergent nature of material is the concept of matter movement and becomings. The intensive movement of matter is the way the world makes and expresses itself, and the way that matter self-organises and engages in spontaneous emergence. It can be described as the invisible and inarticulatable incorporeal affective forces acting on material bodies, involving immanence, expression, self-organisation and emergence, and that which is capable of affecting the mind outside of representation. Significantly, immanence is the inherence of forms of order and not the external imposition of form on matter through causation. This immanent expression of matter movement is processes of self-organisation and the capacities for self-organisation within a relational field. These creative immanent processes produce intensive individuations of bodies, filling the intensive field with intensive emergent bodies.

We can further situate the concept of becoming within this discussion of matter movement. Becoming defines the intensive ontological register, as opposed to the extensive actualised ontological register of Being. A body is perpetually becoming something or something else, ceasing to be what is has been, becoming other. The status of an intensive body is, however, always undecidable, in a superposition of very many potential actual bodies in an intensive becoming, but never being what is actually happening. It is a becoming coincident with and generative of actual Being.[2]

As with matter movement, in becoming there are processes of self-organisation and emergence that build an intensive scaling organisation across the intensive field. Intensive ontogenesis can be understood as an immanent dynamic process of expression across the intensive social field, in which the intensive social field makes continuous processes of unfolding and folding (Deleuze 1990). The flows of matter movement draw upon the differential relations and the distribution of potentials that exist within an intensive field, which leads to a creative (although not linear) extensive production. For Deleuze, the concept of the fold—which comprises continuous folding and unfolding—is the preferred way of understanding processes of becoming between the intensive and the actual and vice versa. In these intensive flows of matter, we have an unfolding and folding, in syntheses that complicate the relay between intensity and actualisation. In expression, the actual unfolds the intensive, and the intensive folds and complicates all forms (Deleuze 1992: 119). This expressive differential relay is always productive, and 'difference is never negative but essentially positive and creative' (Deleuze 1991: 103). Within this framework, intensive ontogenesis creates the world in continuous processes that self-differentiate from intensive singularities of force which emerges across the intensive field, expressing the creativity of ontogenesis in recursive, scaling and self-similar patterns wrought by the unceasing immanent movements of unfolding and folding. Expression in immanent intensive ontogenesis ceaselessly complicates the world, ceaselessly creating and self-organising, uncreating and unself-organising, and then creating and self-organising some more, endless experimentation, evolution and an increase in the dynamic complexity of the world (Deleuze 1992: 119).[3]

Through the concepts of matter movement and becomings we can further understand the complex relationship between the intensive incorporeal register and the extensive material register. The material and corporeal extensive world emerges from the intensive processes and events of the incorporeals and the intensive incorporeal affects and extensive material forms intermingle in any given social field. The relation between the intensive incorporeal and the extensive/actual material is that of an expression of the intensive in the material and this process of expression complicates the world. The extensive material does not come into actual existence without something of the incorporeal inhering in the extensive material, with things having 'a fringe of force of the ideal inevitably surrounding and infiltrating, or even composing matter' (Grosz 2017: 18). This movement and intermingling is that of an enfolding of inherence and corresponding processes of unfolding or expression, involvement and explication, inherence and elaboration and to contract and dilate (Grosz 2017: 87–90). For Massumi, 'the key is always to hold the intensive [virtual] as a co-incident dimension of every event' (Massumi 2013: 18).

5.5 Exploring the Intensive Incorporeals

Intensive incorporeals operate in the manner of the singularities and attractors in the processes and organisation of the intensive ontological register. In this section we examine in detail these intensive incorporeals, focusing specifically upon sensation, intensive bodies, affect-events and affective atmospheres.

5.5.1 Intensive Sensation and Percept

The intensive ontological register is not lived in the same way as the actual register. The actual is lived mediated through consciousness and language; it is lived in feeling and understood in denotation, manifestation and signification. In fundamental contrast, the intensive is lived in sensation and sense (Deleuze 1990). Sensation is intensive: it can be described as the direct unmediated impact upon the central nervous system and as involving the felt immediacy of a real intensive relation and as the first glimmerings of emergence in an intensive field (Deleuze 2006). Hence, an intensive sensation is not feeling (although it is coincident and generative of feeling); rather, it is pre-personal and pre-individual. It can be described a block of intensive sensation of the intensive field directly registering upon an intensive body. It is in sensation that intensive bodies and intensive situations become, and it is through sensation that intensive events occur.

Sensation emerges in blocks in fields of intensive forces, with force closely related to sensation: 'for sensation to exist, a force must be exerted over a body' (Deleuze and Guattari 1994: 56). A block of sensation becomes a percept. Just as we can distinguish between sensation and feeling, we can differentiate between percept and perception, with perceptual sensations serving 'to make perceptible the imperceptible forces that populate the world, affect us, and makes us become' (Deleuze and Guattari 1994: 182). Percepts of sensation are intensive, impersonal and pre-individual and are different from extensive perceptions that are personal feelings that refer to particular things. Hence, intensive sensation and percepts act directly on the central nervous system and mind, operating directly outside of any system of representation. Sensation and percept are also events, with the intensive field and differential relations contracting into sensation and percept in the striking of an intensive event (Massumi 2013: 20). Sensation as an event becomes 'compound of percepts and affects' (Deleuze and Guattari 1994: 175). Put in another way, sensation is an intensive and emergent mixture of numerous percepts and affects. The intensive relational force field conditions compounds of percepts and affects that are 'absolutely self-creative' (Massumi 2013: 20) and continually 'transform themselves' in continuous variation (Deleuze and Guattari 1994: 175). Sensations emerge in self-relations of intensive transition and intensive transformation and as sensational significant events. As intensity, sensation is an excess in material bodies and events, as 'when it [sensation] acquires a body, sensation takes on an excessive and spasmodic appearance exceeding the bounds' (Deleuze 2006: 45). Sensation emerges beyond all representation in an affect and sensation laden excess of materiality.

It is in compositions of blocks of sensation and percepts, in sensations of becomings and in sensation of events, that significant events of sensation come together and populate the intensive field as a plane of sensation. These relations of significant events of sensation compose a plane of sensation that in turn topologically maps relations amongst the significant events of sensation. The consistency of the relations amongst the significant events of sensation is the sense of the plane of sensation (Deleuze 1990). The intensive ontogenesis of expression in the intensive field is 'the production of the world order in sensation, a sensation that transparently covers' all the orders of the intensive field (Grosz 2017: 137). Sensation is mappable in high-dimension topologies of phase space and is capable of understanding in thought and articulatable as attributes of propositions in language. From the perspective of the lived materiality of the intensive social field, sensation is the inherence and subsistence of 'an excess, a sensation in things beyond their current state, the conditions under which things change, the becoming of things, whether material or ideal' (Grosz 2017: 72).

5.5.2 *Intensive Bodies*

The intensive regime composes centres of sensation that develop in expression as organised and relatively persistent intensive bodies. An intensive body is a body before it is organised by actualisation in organic representation, and before any differentiation into a subject-object organisation (Deleuze and Guattari 2017). In intensive affect theory one does not define an intensive body as one would define an extensive body in terms of subjectivity, its form, its organs or its functions. The way to define an intensive body is as an open form of engagement; a set of encounters, affects, transformations, continual variation, potentiality of engagement and connections with other bodies (intensive bodies are also discussed extensively in Deleuze and Guattari (2004, 2017) as 'bodies without organs'). The intensive body is not a thing—rather the nature of the intensive body is 'continually modified by creative encounters the body undergoes with other bodies' (Grosz 2017: 38). It is in constantly changing relations of movement and rest, speeds and slownesses, succession and co-existence (Grosz 2017: 70); consisting of 'axes and vectors, gradients, cinematic movements and dynamic tendencies, in relation to which forms are contingent or accessory' (Deleuze 2006: 45). As speeds and slownesses are pre-personal and sub-representational, they are therefore only understandable in mathematical concepts of axes and vectors as rate of change and also gradients as scaling patterns of rates of change.

Thus, an intensive body's essence is its intensive operation, its degree of power and the identity of a body is endless variation and difference and the increase or decrease of powers of connection and influence. An intensive body is a power to affect and be affected and the powers to which affective encounters bring to affective bodies (Grosz 2017: 76). Such bodies also have moods, capacities and potentials, and a reservoir of unactualised capacities and potentials, all augmented or diminished and as involving intensifications and diminutions of the capacities of life. Hence, it is composed of intensive sensations falling under capacities of encounters and engagements and extensive parts falling under relations on interconnection and interaction. Accordingly, 'what a body is made of is less significant than what it can do' (Grosz 2017: 79).

The intensive body is, however, at one with its transitions (Massumi 2013: 15). It is always in open engagement and encounters with other intensive bodies, with intensive bodies continually engaging in changing relations of affecting and being affected. Nonetheless, amidst these ever-changing relations, an intensive body struggles to preserve its intensive relations of movement and rest, speeds and slownesses. In their open engagements and encounters with other intensive bodies, and in their striving to persist as intensive bodies, they experience increases or decreases in powers and capacities of connection and engagement. Such bodies are both a continuous variation and consistency: pure difference while nonetheless maintaining identity and, further, a phase space portrait with a high dimensionality manifold—a distribution of singularities and a phase space trajectory. Accordingly, the intensive body is 'the preservation of relations of movement and rest even amid the continually changing relations of objects entering and leaving the body' (Grosz 2017: 79).

Furthermore, an intensive body is the set of predicates of an extensive body: what a body can do, and what its particular qualities are. Such bodies are processes of individuation, processes of ontogenesis and latitudes and longitudes that compose a body and in what ways these are capable of being affected: 'latitude is made up of intensive points falling under a capacity, and longitude of extensive parts falling under a relation' (Deleuze and Guattari 2004: 257). It is, of course, not a matter of either an intensive body or an extensive organism body, but of their intermingling: of a body that is more or less intensive and more or less extensive. From the perspective of the embodied life of a social field, there is the intensive body as the excess that subsists and inheres in the actual body, and the issues of the intensive body appearing in the social field. The techniques of affect of intensive bodies are to intensify capacities of transformation and of life.

5.5.3 *Affect-Events*

Affects are the manner by which we can sense and come to understand the dynamics of complex affective assemblages. They can be understood as the block of sensation and sense that is the manner of intensive bodies' engagements, encounters, powers and capacities to interconnect and interact with other intensive bodies. Affects are intensive, impersonal, pre-individual and irreducible to the emotional and the actions and passions of actualised material bodies (Deleuze 1988a, 1990, 1991, 1992; Spinoza 2000. See also Brennan 2004; Massumi 2013, 2015). Rather, they are how intensive bodies act or are acted upon and the manner in which things exist with each other intensely. They are encounters of the forces of the intensive field, the movement of variation of intensive bodies, their constantly changing parts and the modes of flow and their ever-changing relations (Grosz 2017: 79). Hence, affects can be understood as incorporeal movements, intensities of bodies intermingling in open encounters of differential speeds and slownesses, with the intensive bodies being affected by, and affecting, other intensive bodies. Hence, they are neither subjects nor objects, but rather can be understood as an event of a sensational encounter between intensive bodies. 'Affects are events that occur to or between bodies/ideas or that transform bodies/ideas in the intensity of their powers of persistence' (Grosz 2017: 83).

Hence, affects are intensive and incorporeal events; events that are transitions from different points of intensity of processual forces, and of transitions from different thresholds of intensity of open encounters of affect and being affected in intensive bodies. Further, these events are significant in becoming and expression, and they can be understood as bifurcation points in the intensive complex process (concepts we explore further in the next chapter). More specifically, an event is a set of singularities in the field of intensive forces (which can also be described as a distribution of singularities in a complex high dimensionality manifold). Event sets of singularities can be described as 'turning points and points of inflection; bottlenecks, knots, foyers, centers; points of fusion, condensation and boiling; points of tears and joy, sickness and health, hope and anxiety, "sensitive points"' (Deleuze 1990: 55). Significantly, an intensive affect is both an encounter of self-organisation and also a qualitative dimension of bodies encountering of emergence of novel complexity.[4]

We can therefore understand an affect as an intensive event. It is the incorporeal and intensively lived event of transition and crossing of thresholds of becoming and the encounters between bodies affecting and being affected. In their intensity affects are real but not material, and affects are at once a realised relationality and that which exceeds relationality: Thus, there is a 'constitutive duplicity of affect event into co-current relational [extensive] and qualitative [intensive] dimensions' (Massumi 2015: 4). The relationality is that of a field of forces and the exercise of power, and the quality is the affect that resonates from but exceeds material bodies. This field of forces operates in intensity, not as the transition from one extensive state of affairs to another, but rather the incorporeal non-human becoming and event in intensive forces (Deleuze and Guattari 1994: 173). An affect-event is 'an experiential excess over both the sensuous forms involved and the sense modalities' (Massumi 2015: 144). Affect is excessive quality in immanence and intensity, pre-personal, sub-representational and opposed to personal emotions (Michels 2015: 15). It is affect that gets actualised as affections and only then retroactively felt and rationalised.[5]

From the perspective of the lived materiality of the intensive social field, affects are the excesses that subsist and inhere in actual bodies and states of affairs signalling the crossing of intensive thresholds at the level of intensive forces and bodies affecting and being affected. In the language and discourses of the material social field, the intensive affects break the linearity of actual language as 'out of place' 'expressive movements, paralinguistic signs, breaths and screams' (Deleuze 2006: 113). For Deleuze and Guattari 'affects are precisely these non-human becomings of man, just as percepts are non-human landscapes of nature' (Deleuze and Guattari 1994: 169).

5.5.4 *Affective Atmospheres*

In exploring the concept of affects, and particularly their relationship to the courtroom, it is also vital to explore the notion of affective atmospheres. Their provenance derives from Deleuze and Guattari's *What is Philosophy?* in which the reality of the dynamic assembly of affective qualities is frequently conceptualised as 'atmospheres' (Deleuze and Guattari 1994: 96), 'ambient atmospheres' (96) and as 'unhistorical vapours' (100) (see also Anderson 2006, 2009; Michels 2015; Michels and Stayaert 2017; Philippopoulos-Mihalopoulos 2015). In order to understand affective atmospheres, it is crucial to understand the emergence of place. Place emergences in self-assembling blocks of affects-events, which come together as a milieu in which material locations and affective atmospheres emerge. In this, the affective atmospheres are the intensities of experience that occur 'before and alongside the formation of subjectivities, across human and non-human materialities, and in between subject/object distinctions' (Anderson 2009: 78). They emerge between intensive affective bodies and intense affective environments; they are the scene setting of affective qualities and the spatio-temporal realisation of a dynamic assembly of affective qualities (Anderson 2009).

Such atmospheres are the assemblaging of intensive bodies, affects, becomings, spatio-temporal manifestations and dynamic structural (in) stabilities. They find their genesis and operation in the intensive processes of expression and self-organisation. They are marked by processes of cohering and inhering, continuous change and resonating spatio-temporal intensities. They are the affectual bloom of a processual incorporeal materialism and form of belonging (Massumi 2013). Indeed, the 'embracing atmosphere ... is also at the very heart of what happens ... [and] an affective tonality is what we normally call a mood' (Massumi 2013: 66). As well as a mood, affective atmospheres are also eventual, scattered with significant transitional points between the differential elements that set the conditions for its self-organisation and emergence (Massumi 2013: 20). Not only are affective atmospheres the spatio-temporal location of events, they are also that which further cohere the affect-events into an emerging macro scale climate. As Massumi notes, it is 'the affective tonality that produces the resemblance between the events by holding them together in itself' (Massumi 2013: 124). They form as the intensive excess of affect in self-organisation and emergence of the atmosphere (Massumi 2013: 18). Pragmatically, it is through affective atmospheres 'how lived abstraction can be felt in our embodied animal life' (Massumi 2013: 18). Affective atmospheres can be understood as the scaling up of micro affects and events into a more intensively complex climate, which is spatially and temporally located, which is also constantly changing and shifting. In this sense, it can also be conceptualised as a field.

5.6 The Logic of Sense: Affect and Events in Language

As we have now set out the intensive incorporeals, we return to explore the notion of sense in a little more detail. Sense is a complex incorporeal, and the logic of sense is key to the operation of the problem field and the operation of the intensive ontological order. Sense is pervasive in Deleuze's ontology of affect, and it is the incorporeal entity that does much of the work of the creative relay between the intensive and the actual. Sense simultaneously operates in the intensive, operates at the border between the intensive and the actual and it appears in the actual. The border between the intensive and the actual is the border between intensive expression and material bodies and continues into the border between the interconnections and interactions of semiotic regimes and the material regimes. Sense appears in the actual of language and discourse.[6] Sense is always the logic of sense—a logic of the intensive, the problem field and the genesis of sense in expression, language and discourse.[7] Sense is not of the logic of representation, and it has nothing to do with denotation, manifestation and signification which are representational.

To explore the logic of sense further, we break it down into ten interrelated propositions:

1. Problematic: Sense is in the intensive problem field. Indeed, sense is the problem field itself: 'sense is the genesis of the problematic' (1994: 201). It is in the distribution of singularities in the high dimensionality manifold problem field. As such, sense is what makes up the intensive problematic of the problem field (Deleuze 1994: 23).
2. Logical and Meaningful Relations of Incorporeals: Sense is the logical and meaningful incorporeal relations in the intensive. It is the relations of sensation, intensive bodies, intensive affects, affective atmospheres and of incorporeal organisation in dynamic

multiplicities of incorporeal events. Sense in the incorporeal relations is an alignment of intensive bodies and incorporeal compositions of sense.

3. Conditions under which Things Become: These multiplicity relations of incorporeals are the conditions under which things change and the becoming of the world, and the conditions under which sense is expressed and sense sayable in language and discourse. Incorporeal events come to transform something, produce sense and enable something to mean something.
4. Sense is Emergent: Sense is an immanent, emergent self-organisation of a complex composite of sensation, intensive bodies, affect-events and affective atmospheres. This composite is genitive and is the genesis of the becoming of the world and of the composition of sense in expression, language and discourse. Sense appears in expression and as that which is expressed in language, propositions and verbs (Deleuze 1990). What language expresses is incorporeal, a process, an event, a change of state, a modification. Sense in thought and sense in language is the intensive and incorporeal expression of intensive relations, events and transformations. It is the intensive composition of intensive bodies and sense in intensive expression, and it is the field of singularities that condition the possibilities of sense-making. It is in expression that sensation and affect can enter language: 'There is sensation, then there are significant events of sensation that are rendered articulatable as sense in language' (Grosz 2017: 32).
5. Sense-Making Composition: Sense is sense-making through the intensive and in the problematic as the self-organisation and emergence of sense and intensive composition. Sense is in events making a composition of bodies and senses, the sayable of an utterance and not the materiality of the saying (Grosz 2017: 43). Sense-making in the problematic is the genesis of solutions—the conditions of the problem that provide solutions with their sense and the sense which continues to subsist in actual solutions. It is at the border between the intensive and the actual, between intensive expression and material bodies and continues into the border between the interconnections and interactions of semiotic regimes and the material regimes.
6. Capable of Transmission: Sense is an incorporeal affect-event, a transformation articulable in language and capable of transmission.

It is emitted or erupts at the surface between expression and the material, and when expressed in language and discourse is of signs. Signs are extra-propositional, an excess of intensities and 'the true element of theatre' (Deleuze 1994: 28). Making sense is the invention of language and of the means by which the incorporeal sense can become 'articulatable and capable of transmission' (Grosz 2017: 43). We know of events only to the extent that language enables us to invent propositions which contain some of the sense of the event itself (Grosz 2017: 43).

7. Excess (Adherence): Sense appears in language and discourse as an intensive excess, and which adheres to language and discourse as excess of incorporeal affect. Hence it appears in language and discourse as the inherence and subsistence of 'an excess, a sense in things beyond their current state, the conditions under which things change, the becoming of things, whether material or ideal' (Grosz 2017: 72).
8. Truth (Problematics): The making of intensive sense in language and discourse is the making of sense in the intensive problematic. The logic of sense extends to the genesis and production of the true. For Deleuze 'sense is the genesis of the problematic of the true', it is 'the genesis of the true' and 'is the composition of truth' (Deleuze 1994: 201). Sense is the production of the true and false by means of problems. A proposition can be true or false if it has intensive sense (Deleuze 1994: 210; Grosz 2017: 43).
9. Speculative Pragmatics to Produce Truth: Sense-making of the intensive problematic and genesis of intensive theatrical signs becomes in the intensive social field, ultimately, 'the speculative pragmatic power to produce truth' (Massumi 1992: 175).
10. Common Sense, Good Sense: Affective sense-making and the generation of truths as inventive sense is sharply contrasted by Deleuze with the invocation of common sense and good sense (Deleuze 1994: 141–221). In Deleuze's logic of sense, common sense and good sense are actual, representational and extensive. They disfigure and block intensive and creative sense-making and the genesis of truth. Common sense and good sense model identity as recognition, judgement as analogy, imaginary oppositions and perceived similitude (Deleuze 1994: 182). Common sense deploys as that which everyone knows, and good sense deploys as how everyone thinks and how common sense is measured and regulated. In short,

common sense and good sense are judgement in the logic of representation; this is not to be confused with the logic of sense.[8]

5.7 Intensive Field as a Problem Field

Now we have examined the intensive incorporeals, we can return to the consideration of the intensive field and understand that it is an ontogenetic field of felt relations of becomings, expressive self-organisation, sensation and sense, intensive bodies and affects-events. So much of the intensive field and its workings can be grasped by a participating intensive body in sensation, sense and affect. The intensive field may also be grasped in thought as its own doubled ontogenesis as not only an intensive field of sensation and affect, but also as the problematic field of intensive ontogenesis (Deleuze 1990, 1994; Deleuze and Guattari 1994, 2004; Delanda 2000, 2013; Byrne and Callaghan 2014). The event is always an affect, but the incorporeal event is also a set of singularities in a mappable intensive field: 'The mode of the event is in the problematic' (Deleuze 1990: 56).

The intensive field of forces is not amenable to theorisation in reductionist or representational frames; rather it can be theorised and understood in terms of phase space (Massumi 2002). Phase space is a way of mapping complex dynamic systems in what is known as high dimensionality manifolds, plotting instantaneous composite points for the variables of the complex system, thereby populating the problem space with a distribution of singular points that indicate significant events and bifurcation points. In this, it is events that develop the conditions of the problem field, as it is the significant events within the intensive field that condition the presence and distribution of singularities within the problematic field (Deleuze 1990: 57). In terms of the intensive field as a problem field, 'we can speak of events only as singularities deployed in a problematic field, in the vicinity of which solutions are organised' (Deleuze 1990: 56). The eventful problem space is also the mapping of sense in the intensive field: sense is expressed in language as attributes of propositions, but sense is seen most clearly as the distribution of singularities in a high dimensionality problem space: 'sense is a method of question and answer that doubles that of problems in the inquisitory that grounds the problematic' (Deleuze 1990: 59). Thus, solutions do not suppress problems, but it is precisely the conditions of the problems that provide solutions with their sense and which continue to subsist in actual solutions.

In non-representational affect theory what is fundamental to the conceptualisation of incorporeal materialism is the problem field. The concept of the problem field is fundamental because it is at once ontological and epistemological. For Deleuze's incorporeal materialism of affect 'the problematic is both an objective category of knowledge and a perfectly objective kind of being' (Deleuze 1990: 54). The problem field is ontologically real in both the ontogenesis of the world and in the ontogenesis of thinking (Deleuze 1990: 107; 1994). In terms of our consideration of the affective incorporeals, the problem field is fundamental because it is the conditioning of the very possibility of sense-making. Crucial to the conceptual framework of *Difference and Repetition* and *Logic of Sense* (particularly chapter 'Ninth Series on the Problematic') is that 'sense is the problem itself' (Deleuze 1994: 2).

To briefly indicate the elements necessary to machine the problem field and the production of sense there is needed: a high dimensionality manifold, a distribution of continuous singularities, events, multiplicities, a quasi-cause, a problem field and a problematic, along with the production of sense and the eventful production of instances of potential solutions (Deleuze 1990, 1994). The conceptualisation of a distribution of singularities in a high dimensionality in the deployment of a topology of the generation of sense that is itself a precursor process for the production of sense: the topology makes something invisible and nonsensical in the world become visible and sensible. The problem field is a topologically embedded 'impersonal and pre-individual transcendental field' (Deleuze 1990: 102) of the play of the distribution of singularities in a high dimensionality manifold. The existence and distribution of singularities 'are relations to the problematic field' (Deleuze 1990: 107). In this 'we can speak of events only as singularities deployed in a problematic field, in the vicinity of which the solutions are organised' (Deleuze 1990: 56). In the problem field, in struggling with solutions and the production of sense, it is a matter of encountering pre-personal singularities and an intensive field of the becoming of problems. In the becoming of problems it is the intensive events that are the conditions that determine problems (Grosz 2017: 145) and events that condition the possible production of sense.

5.8 Planes of Composition and Organisation

In this final section, we turn to the plane of composition, which is a composition of intensive bodies and incorporeal sense. In Deleuze and Guattari's new materialist philosophy the social field consists of three planes of framing: a virtual plane of philosophy, an intensive plane of composition and an extensive plane of organisation. The three planes span and frame chaos, but in very different ways. In affective assemblage theory the concern is with the spanning and framing of the social in the two planes of composition and organisation and the relations between the two. The extensive social field is the vernacular social field of everyday experience that is actualised out of the intensive social in stable conditions, but which is also counter-actualised under unstable conditions back into the intensive social field. Accordingly, our particular focus is on the intensive plane of composition and intensive social field, with the extensive plane of organisation, dominant emotions and representation being derivative of the processes of the intensive plane of social composition.

The plane of composition is generated from the immanent forces of the intensive ontogenetic register and problem field. The plane of composition is thus the composition of all the sensations, senses, intensive bodies and affect-events, and the plane orientates the becomings in the intensive field. It is composed immanently and transversally organised. The plane of composition is, of course, also expressed in the problem space of the intensive field that draws a plane of the problematic across the high dimensionality manifold. The intensive draws together affective atmospheres and sense, composing together intensive discursive elements and material elements, incorporeal elements and corporeal elements, dynamically meshed continuous multiplicities, the plane of the abstract composition of affective senses and human and non-human becomings. This affective and intensively composed meshed plane of composition is of emergent fragments of visibilities and sayabilities becoming perceptible. The plane of composition holds together in an intensive dynamic consistency, confronting chaos and rendering chaos consistent.[9]

Hence, the plane of composition is an intensive social field. It is a battle of forces, a field of sensation and affect, an intensive superposition of states and bodies co-existing at once, where bodies directly speak, and words and things intermingle, affects are unpredictable and outcomes non-linear, and a cascading unravelling of the intensive field into actualised bodies and states of affairs. In Deleuze's materialist philosophy, drawing and composing a plane of composition is physical, chemical, biological and ecological, but also associated with social and cultural practices of art, drama and ritual (Deleuze and Guattari 1994).

The intensive plane of composition is always doubled and co-exists with the extensive plane of organisation. However, the plane of composition of the intensive field is very different from the plane of organisation of the actualised world (Deleuze and Guattari 1994). The latter is a transcendent plan of the actual world, drawn within a reductionist and representational frame. It is the plan that has been taken up in modern science and modern models of the social field and it is a plan of the world that proceeds through hypothesis, tests, confirmations, results, functions, comprehensibility and the possible. The plan of organisation is the actual stratification and coding that is deposited into extensive existence out of now finished and cancelled out intensive processes into states of affairs and stable attractors. We can understand it as the plane of dominant perceptions and affections, of common sense and good sense, of emotions and feelings (as opposed to affects and affective sense). It is the plane of organisation that grounds representation, with resemblance, linear causation, analogy, customs and laws. Furthermore, it is the default framework for understanding the social field, as has been the case with understandings of social and justice institutions such as the criminal courts.

In contrast to the plan of composition, the plane of organisation is the turning away from chaos and intensity; it 'relinquishes the infinite in order to gain reference' (Deleuze and Guattari 1994: 197) and it is the conventional everyday and 'an umbrella to shield us against chaos' (202). On every plane of composition, a hard crust of a plane of organisation will be forming, and in every plane of organisation the strata and coding will continually be broken apart and intensified by the underlying and persisting plane of composition.

5.8.1 *Plane-ing*

For Deleuze and Guattari the planes are both ontological and epistemological. However, the intensive and the plane of composition are a very different ontological register to that of the actual and the plane of organisation. Almost all the taken-for-granted orientations of the actual simply do not hold in the intensive. Thus, for example, in the intensive the taken-for-granted subject/object divide does not hold, nor does the taken-for-granted linearity of cause and effect. However, this does not mean that there are not ways for navigating an intensive field and composing a plane of composition. Although participation and interventions in an intensive field is a somewhat risky undertaking, and there must be more modest and careful methods and goals than those for organising an actual field and plane of organisation.[10]

5.9 Conclusion

To frame the social field as an intensive field, and to frame a social institution, such as the criminal courts, as an intensive field, is to fundamentally re-orientate criminological and legal studies as facing the intensive field. It is also to fundamentally re-orientate criminology and legal studies to the art of the composition of a plane of composition. This in turn re-orientates the problematic of the intensive social field as one that is fundamentally political and aesthetic. It is also to re-orientate participation in the criminal justice system as a mode of composition and as best understood as a political and aesthetic problematic and practice.

Notes

1. The interaction between the actual and intensive is explored at various points in the data chapters. See for example the discussion in Sect. 3.2.1.
2. Various intensive superpositions are discernible within the barrister data. These include their perspectives concerning conviction rates (Sect. 2.3) and jury decision-making processes (Sect. 4.3).
3. Barristers could be seen to understand, and place significant emphasis on the importance of, emergence, self-organisation and non-linearity within the rape courtroom assemblage. Indeed, they demonstrated a preference for bottom-up and emergent solutions. See for example the discussions in Sects. 2.3, 3.2.1, 3.2.3, 3.2.4, 3.3, 4.2, 4.5 and 4.6.
4. Drawing upon the barristers' perspectives, as well as law and policy documents, throughout the data chapters we identify and map various attractors and singularities of the rape courtroom affective assemblage. These in turn could be seen to influence barristers' techniques of affect and the drawing of a plane of composition. Through this, we can start to understand the problem field (both actual and intensive) and the phase space of the rape courtroom assemblage. The key attractors and singularities we explore are conviction rates (Sect. 2.3); the jury (see in particular Sects. 3.2.1, 3.2.2, and 4.5); consent (Sect. 3.2.1); judge's directions (Sect. 3.2.1); common sense (Sects. 3.2.1, 3.2.2 and 3.2.3); not over-complicating the trial (Sect.

3.2.3); the reality of practice (Sect. 3.2.3); real life (Sect. 3.2.2); rape myths and misconceptions (Sects. 3.3 and 4.4); courtroom tactics and winning cases (Sect. 4.2); embodied, live and emotional courtroom performances (Sects. 4.3 and 4.4); and the lack of independent evidence and the importance of the complainant's testimony (Sect. 4.4).

5. Affects assumed a critical role in the rape courtroom assemblage and fundamentally informed and inspired trial practice. Barristers clearly appreciated the capacity of the body to affect and be affected and were concerned with marshalling affects and engaging in techniques of affect in order to transform the jury. We explore this in considerable detail in both Chaps. 3 and 4. See for example Sects. 3.2, 3.3, 4.2, 4.3, 4.4 and 4.6.
6. We explore moments where sense could be seen to enter into discourse and language in Sect. 4.6, in relation to eruptive expressions within complainant testimony.
7. The empirical data suggests that barristers had a strong and intuitive intensive sense of the rape courtroom assemblage, and that this fundamentally informed their perspectives on and use of law and policy reforms and practice. We discuss this throughout Chaps. 2, 3 and 4. See for example Sects. 2.3, 3.2.1, 3.4, 4.2 and 4.4.
8. Common sense was a key attractor for advocates within the rape courtroom assemblage. However, this frequently sat in tension with their intensive sense of the trial. See for example Sects. 3.2.1, 3.2.2 and 4.4.
9. Rendering perceptible the various intensive and incorporeal forces and relationships between the heterogeneous bodies within the rape courtroom assemblage is a key aspect of the analysis throughout the data chapters. But see for example Sects. 2.3 and 3.2.4.
10. A key argument developed throughout the data chapters is that barristers are involved in drawing a plane of composition and this fundamentally drives their courtroom practices. We also highlight how complainants can also be seen to be engaged in drawing a plane of composition in Sect. 4.6.

References

Alliez, E. (2004). *The Signature of the World: What Is Deleuze & Guattari's Philosophy?* London: Continuum.

Anderson, B. (2006). Becoming and Being Hopeful: Towards a Theory of Affect. *Environmental and Planning D: Society and Space, 24*(5), 733–752.

Anderson, B. (2009). Affective Atmospheres. *Emotion, Space and Society, 2*(2), 77–81.

Brennan, T. (2004). *Transmission of Affect.* New York: Cornell University Press.

Byrne, D., & Callaghan, G. (2014). *Complexity Theory and the Social Sciences.* Abingdon: Routledge.

Delanda, M. (2000). *A Thousand Years of Nonlinear History*. New York: Zone Books.
Delanda, M. (2013). *Intensive Science, Virtual Philosophy*. London: Bloomsbury.
Deleuze, G. (1988a). *Spinoza: Practical Philosophy*. San Francisco: City Lights.
Deleuze, G. (1988b). *Foucault*. London: Continuum.
Deleuze, G. (1990). *Logic of Sense*. London: Athlone Press.
Deleuze, G. (1991). *Bergsonism*. New York: Zone Books.
Deleuze, G. (1992). *Expressionism in Philosophy: Spinoza*. New York: Zone Books.
Deleuze, G. (1994). *Difference & Repetition*. London: Athlone Press.
Deleuze, G. (2006). *Francis Bacon: Logic of Sensation*. London: Continuum.
Deleuze, G., & Guattari, F. (1994). *What Is Philosophy?* London: Verso.
Deleuze, G., & Guattari, F. (2004). *A Thousand Plateaus*. London: Continuum.
Deleuze, G., & Guattari, F. (2017). *Anti-Oedipus*. London: Bloomsbury.
Grosz, E. (2017). *The Incorporeal: Ontology, Ethics, and the Limits of Materialism*. New York: Columbia University Press.
Massumi, B. (1992). *A User's Guide to Capitalism and Schizophrenia: Deviations from Deleuze and Guattari*. Massachusetts: MIT Press.
Massumi, B. (2002). *Parables for the Virtual: Movement, Affect, Sensation*. Durham: Duke University Press.
Massumi, B. (2013). *Semblance & Event: Activist Philosophy and the Occurrent Arts*. Massachusetts: MIT Press.
Massumi, B. (2015). *Politics of Affect*. Cambridge: Polity.
Michels, C. (2015). Researching Affective Atmospheres. *Geographica Helvetica, 70*(4), 255–263.
Michels, C., & Stayaert, C. (2017). By Accident and by Design: Composing Affective Atmospheres in an Urban Art Intervention. *Organisation, 24*(1), 79–104.
Philippopoulos-Mihalopoulos, A. (2015). *Spatial Justice, Body, Lawscape, Atmosphere*. Abingdon: Routledge.
Spinoza, B. (2000). *Ethics*. Oxford: Oxford University Press.

CHAPTER 6

Complexity Theory, Deleuze and Guattari's Affective Assemblage Theory and the Courtroom as Affective Assemblage

Abstract This chapter continues the philosophically advanced exploration of the theoretical framework by focusing upon two major theories of the organisation of complex social assemblages. The first theory is that of complexity science and complexity theory, with the central concepts of self-organisation, emergence, order-out-of-chaos and transformation in social organisation. The second is the assemblage theory developed by Deleuze and Guattari on conceptualising social organisation in terms of the doubly articulated semiotic regime and material regime and in terms of operations of territorialisation, deterritorialisation and reterritorialisation. In conclusion, we consider what it means to reconceptualise the courtroom as an affective assemblage.

Keywords Complexity theory and science • Affective assemblages • Territorialisation • Deterritorialisation • Reterritorialisation • Semiotic and material regimes

6.1 Introduction

The previous chapter on Deleuze's materialist philosophy of the intensive affective social field and the plane of composition proposed an incorporeal materialist framework. This incorporeal materialism was seen to be a materialist ontology but one that posited the need for incorporeal intensi-

A. Carline et al., *Rape and the Criminal Trial*, Palgrave Socio-Legal Studies, https://doi.org/10.1007/978-3-030-38684-9_6

ties and events to adequately account for the ontogenesis of complex material systems. Incorporeals were specified as real in an ontological register of immanence as sensations, bodies, affects-events, affective atmospheres, sense, becomings and transformations and the intensive plane of composition. A non-representational problem space for modelling such intensive processes and events was also specified as high dimensionality manifolds and the dynamic distribution of singularities in the manifold.

The overall aim of this chapter is to further explore the intensive social field and to conceptualise the courtroom as an affective assemblage. This is to advance into Deleuze and Guattari's affective social assemblage theory. A crucial part of assemblage theory is to understand the genesis and operation of the affective assemblage as a complex system. Thus, the discussion of complexity theory is to address the central underlying assumptions of affective assemblage theory. However, this discussion of complexity science may also allow a deepened understanding of the previous chapter's intensive affective field, which may also be understood as a complex system. In many respects, complexity science comes to substantiate materialist philosophical speculation regarding incorporeals in complex systems.

This chapter explores the organisation and transformation of complex social assemblages and considers two major theories, with the first underlying the second. The first theory of the organisation of complex social assemblages is complexity science and complexity theory, with central concepts of self-organisation, emergence, order-out-of-chaos and transformation in social organisation. The second is assemblage theory developed by Deleuze and Guattari (2017, 1986, 2004, 1994), which derives in many respects from Deleuze's materialist philosophy of affect and sense and from Deleuze and Guattari's engagement with complexity science and theory. Deleuze and Guattari's affective assemblage theory draws together a theory of the intensive field of affect, and a theory of a complex field of self-organisation and emergence and further consolidates the theory of intensive emergence by articulating a framework for theorising social organisation. Social organisation is theorised in terms of the intensive field and self-organisation and emergence in a dynamic assemblage organisation of a complex interplay of a semiotic regime of expression and a material regime of bodies, earth and technology, all run through by ceaseless processes of territorialisation, deterritorialisation and reterritorialisation. Taken together these three takes on an affective intensive ontogenesis of the social field—(1) Deleuze's materialist philosophy of affect and sense,

(2) complexity science and theory and (3) Deleuze and Guattari's affective social assemblage theory—constitute a depth to the theoretical framework adequate to the re-orientation of criminology and legal studies to re-address the problematic of sexual violence and criminal justice, and the dynamics of court rooms, in ways that are novel and productive.

6.2 Complexity Science and Complex Systems

Complexity science has developed a set of discoveries and new scientific concepts for understanding the organisation and operation of complex systems (Bak et al. 1987; Gleick 1987; Prigogine and Stengers 1989; Waldrop 1992; Lorenz 1993; Coveney and Highfield 1995; Kauffman 1995, 2000; Bak 1996; Holland 1999; Morin 2007, 2008; Scheffer 2009; Byrne and Callaghan 2014; Capra 2014; Colander and Kupers 2014). Complexity science is characterised by the discovery of infinitely complex chaos, real-but-not-actual attractors, bifurcation points, order-out-of-chaos, self-organisation, emergence, dissipative structures and self-organising criticality. Thus, building on these core concepts, complexity theory becomes organised on a systemic meta-concept of transformation as definitional of all complex systems in respect not only of their self-organisation but also of their emergence-out-of-chaos and in the dynamics of their operations.

In complexity science the world of physics and chemistry is made up of complex systems, the world of biology is made up of complex adaptive systems that evolve and the social world is made up of complex adaptive systems that socially evolve. The difference between complex systems and complex adaptive systems is simply that the latter demonstrates self-organisation that adapts and that evolution can operate on those adaptations.

6.2.1 Discovering the Incorporeals

One of the striking features of complexity science of the last 50 years is that it has developed concepts and scientific technologies to explore the intensive problem field of complex material systems, and that it has discovered and conceptualised many immanent incorporeal intensities and events. Complexity science is remarkable because it has discovered, mapped and conceptualised precisely those intensities that incorporeal materialist philosophy found itself necessarily to philosophically conceptualise. The language of complexity science and theory for these incorporeals is specific to their own undertaking, but the concepts discovered and developed in complex material systems by complexity science (and theory) accord and chime strikingly with the incorporeal concepts of incorporeal materialist philosophy.

Attractors and Bifurcation Points

In complexity science and theory, the operation of real-but-not-actual attractors is crucial to understanding a complex material system. As we note and explained in Chap. 2, there are various categories of complex attractors. These include simple state and cycle attractors. Crucially, what complexity science and theory has discovered and conceptualised are chaotic attractors, which we explore below.

Bifurcation points are that point at which a trajectory of a complex system becomes under the force of a new attractor, whether stable, cycle or chaotic. At this critical point the complex system jumps attractors, and a new organisation, operation and future of a complex system opens out. In complex systems the bifurcation point is characteristically non-linear, abrupt phase shifts and frequently the harbinger of radical novelty and creativity. Classic bifurcation points in complexity science are freezing and boiling points in liquids. Yet bifurcation points can be emergent, such as the transition to a dissipative system (an open system which operates far-from-equilibrium) (Prigogine and Stengers 1989). In very many respects, the complexity science bifurcation point is what we have already encountered in affect theory of an event.[1]

High Dimensionality Manifolds and Distribution of Attractors

Complexity science maps into a system's high dimensionality manifold a phase space portrait of how the complex system changes and transforms over time and the regions of the phase space that the ongoing process of the complex system is attracted to. In mapping the phase space portrait of a repeating simple system, what emerges is the inherence in the organisation and operation of a system of attractors, which although not identifiable from an observation of the actualised material system, does nonetheless condition the organisation and operation of the system. An observable feature of complex systems is that they are in seemingly perpetual change, with sudden and sometimes dramatic transformations and profound observational difficulties of system predictability. When such systems are mapped in a phase space portrait, they follow a trajectory that never repeats itself and remains in perpetual change. However, the phase trajectories do not distribute randomly through the phase space, but rather generate patterns that repeat-but-never-actually repeat in phase space. Many complex systems turn out to occupy extremely limited regions of their phase space and are attracted in a fuzzy but insistent regions of phase space. The fuzzy insistent attraction to particular regions of a system's phase space are its chaotic attractors. As in the phase space portrait of the famous Lorenz attractor, a complex system may occupy particular trajectories and regions of its full phase space and show never-exactly-repeating but characteristic dramatic system attractors. Amongst the trajectories across, and between attractors, bifurcation points of fundamental system organisation and operation change. In particular, complex systems can combine a simultaneous and conflicting attraction of a large array of mixed stable attractors, cyclical attractors and chaotic attractors, all mapping out in the system trajectories a complex persistent yet never strictly repeating pattern.[2]

Order-out-of-Chaos and Self-Organisation

In complexity science, chaos has a broad range of modes of operating and is conceptualised very differently to the ancient and everyday notion of a state of disorder in need of transcendent hylomorphic ordering. There is the chaos theory concept of chaos as deterministic and sensitivity to initial conditions (Gleick 1987; Lorenz 1993). This concept, although allowing for a rich understanding of immense fractal patterning and creative folding in chaos, always tends towards entropy and the second law of thermodynamics. Rather, in complexity science it is the counter-intuitive and counter-entropic potentiality of chaos that is brought forward as the defining feature. Chaos is not a state of disorder, but rather an infinite matter movement of processes of inmixing of disorder and order on all scales (Gleick 1987). Complexity chaos is a creative chaos which is in part counter-entropic along with being entropic. It is the processes discovered in complexity science of order-out-of-chaos (Prigogine and Stengers 1989), the creativity of the edge of chaos (Kauffman 1995, 2000) and a dimension of chaos that is generative of self-organised criticality (Bak et al. 1987). It is a chaos that is creative. Order-out-of-chaos is order that is not imposed on the world, but that which spontaneously develops and creates precisely in conditions that had been previously set aside as the definition of the absence of creation and order (Prigogine and Stengers 1989). In the parlance of the previous chapter, complex systems arise and self-organise in an intensive field of forces of composition, and complex systems are their own intensive problem field, perpetually self-organising and reciprocally changing their problem field.

Self-organisation is the idea that these forces of order-out-of-chaos are a creative process that automatically develops complex processual relationalities, dynamic patterns and significant intensive events. Complex systems come into existence through immanent processes in disorganised matter-energy-information flows. At one level, all complex systems owe their material existence to the thermodynamic energy of the sun, and consequently those complex systems are thermodynamically powered by flows of matter. Complex systems are thus open to matter-energy-information flows, and these flows will push a complex system to operate far-from-equilibrium (with the instabilities this brings). Immanent processes in the matter-energy-information flows spontaneously bring into existence complex systems, organising the flows out of chaos counter-entroprically to create organisation. This counter-entropic organisation may persist for some time, perhaps developing robust secondary organisation. Yet just as easily as it came into existence, the complex system organisation can become unstable, and it can disappear back into the disorganised chaotic flows from which it came.

It is complexity that is immanent in the disorganised flows and which creates organisation and structure of the world. Complexity is the organisation of all levels and stages of complex system and operation, but complexity starts with a relationality and thermodynamically driven recursive operations of repeated connections and inter-relations between elements, interconnections and inter-relations. The creativity of complexity starts in the immanent zone of organisation through interconnections and inter-relations.

Emergence, Dissipative Structures and Self-Organising Criticality

Emergence is the idea that in self-organising systems that create new dynamic order that what emerges is something of significantly novel systemic qualities and capacities, that are fundamentally more than a mere sum of their parts as they were before the systemic self-organisation processes (Kauffman 1995, 2000). In the creativity of complexity there is no top-down design, imposition of form or central control. Rather, the processes are immanent and self-organising, transforming energy into organisation, and then self-organising that organisation with another organisation, to create yet more organisation. The self-organisation in complex systems starts at the micro-molecular level, assembling micro elements, connections and inter-relations, which are then organised by complexity in more complex ways. However, this micro-molecular 'grass-roots' creativity is continually happening in complex systems and can flourish.

Complexity also has a meso level of creative organisation. Amongst the self-organising micro-molecular processes creating micro-molecular elements, interconnections and inter-relations, complexity introduces dynamic network interconnections and interactions that establish more complex relationality and consistencies amongst the molecular interconnections and inter-relations. Complex systems are defined by what Ilya Prigogine discovered and termed 'dissipative structure'—outbreaks of dynamic stability in far-from-equilibrium matter-energy flows that organised a systemic structure in the flows, but exhibiting multiple potential stable dissipative structures to which it could transform (and also just simply collapse back into chaos).

The concept of dissipative structures concerns the self-organisation of complex systems and derives from Ilya Prigogine's discovery in thermodynamic chemical conditions that dynamic and spontaneous order does emerge under far-from-equilibrium conditions (Prigogine and Stengers 1989). This far-from-equilibrium order is a dynamic holding-together of the system in an ordering of perpetual transformation in an intensive systemic regime precariously bordering both the edge of order and the edge of chaos. By virtue of their immanent micro-molecular self-organisation, immanent dynamic dissipative structure of self-organisation and the immensely strong conception of emergence, complex systems are organisationally open systems. That is to say that they do not have one closed systemic organisation, upon which the system is duly organised on, or is dead. Rather, complex systems may have multiple potential alternative organisations that the complex system could 'choose' to switch to at any one point in time. Furthermore, the operation of dissipative structure emergence generates continuous creativity in novel emergent organisations for the complex system.

Dissipative structures can form stable patterns and shapes and display a systemic dynamic consistency and systemic qualities and capacities. This dynamic consistency between the attractors is, of course, the system's dissipative structure. The organisation and operation of a complex system is the dynamic conditioning of the actual complex system of an immanent dissipative structure in the field of its composing forces.

Self-organised criticality is a discovery and scientific concept closely linked to order-out-of-chaos, self-organisation and emergence at the edge-of-chaos dissipative structures. It was the 1987 paper 'Self-Organised Criticality' by Bak, Ting and Wiesenfeld (1987) that marked the discovery, although ideas about the self-organising process evolving to edge of chaos have also been extensively explored by the biologist Stuart Kauffman (1995, 2000, 2008). Self-organised criticality is something that emerges in non-equilibrium non-linear dynamic systems. In such systems there are located (intensively, in phase space) a chaotic attractor that is on a critical point of a phase transition between order and chaos. Self-organisation tunes the non-equilibrium system towards the critical point of a self-organisation at the edge-of-chaos phase transition. This self-organising tuning prompts the system into the zone of tapping the creativity of self-organisation and emergence that is emitted from a complex system at the edge of chaos. Self-organised criticality is, therefore, understood in complexity science as one concept of related concepts that capture the creativity of the edge of chaos dissipative structure of self-organisation, emergence and complexity in nature.[3]

Discovery of Systemic Transformation, Adaption and Evolution
The creativity of complexity immanently interconnects complex systems into other complex systems, creating new interconnections. These new interconnections generate new interactions between interconnected complex systems and a further complex dynamic organisation is generated. New ways of organising and emergent organisational innovations can emerge, such as relation of symbiosis between complex systems. Further, complex systems interconnecting and interacting with other complex systems will become nested, with increased complexity. Nested complex systems are forever creating new niches for new complex systems to emerge and occupy.

Complex systems organised by dissipative structure emergence and nested new capacities can become adaptive and to self-organise macro emergent creative enabling constraints. They can also respond to changes in its nested complex environment by experimenting and changing its own interconnections, interactions or organisation, in different ways. Complex system adaptation can generate new alternative arrangements by experimenting with local interconnections, interactions and organisation and then take up a self-organising selection and rejection operation on these adaptations. Evolution is, of course, the prototype of the adaptation process. Complex systems that are not biological reproduce from time to time, and as such can also evolve. Perhaps most significantly of all, the organisational openness of complex systems allows us to think about transformation in complex systems.

6.2.2 Complexity Science

Thus, in complexity science the key terms for self-organising and emergent incorporeality are attractors, bifurcation points and dissipative structures (with these corresponding to affects, events and the intensive plane of composition). In this discovery and with the conceptualisation of attractors, events and dissipative structures, complexity science and theory presuppose an immanent intensive field of relational creative forces and processual differentials, which they conceptualise in a (frequently computer-generated topology of the field of forces) high dimensionality 'flat' manifold. This is organised by a dynamic distribution of attractors that hold together a dissipative structure precisely by means of the structures continuous transformation and the dramatic bifurcation points that roll through the system transformation. In this sense, the complexity science conceptualisation of a complex system appears as a mathematically rigorous precise analogue of incorporeal materialist philosophy. This analogue includes shared concepts of a self-organising field of emergence, a complex problem space of distributions of intensive singularities and affects and of the processes of intensive becomings and events.

6.3 Complexity Theory and Complex Social Systems

Complexity theory, thus, forms a set of general concepts for understanding the organisation and operation of complex systems. The theory converts scientific concepts into general theoretical concepts, which we have explored (i.e. infinitely complex chaos, real-but-not-actual attractors, bifurcation points, order-out-of-chaos, self-organisation, emergence, dissipative structures and self-organising criticality). Importantly, complex systems are considered to not be amenable to reductionist analytical science and social science and not amenable to an orthodox representational logic more generally. This involves a shift from a now surpassed modernist paradigm to a complexity paradigm (Capra and Mattei 2015).

Despite the existence of a broad consensus across complexity theory that the world is largely constituted in complex systems and that these complex systems are open, self-organising and emergent, there is an important diversity within complexity theory. The French philosopher of complexity Morin introduced a distinction between restricted complexity and general complexity, that has subsequently been adopted widely as a way to understand some of the different strands of complexity theory (Byrne and Callaghan 2014). Morin's framing of the binary appears to function to put a maximal distance between the restricted complexity that had come to characterise the US Santa Fe theories and their advancement into computational complexity and the formalisation of complexity, and a general philosophical complexity that stayed true to the more open and philosophical concerns of General Systems Theory and an open ontology of complexity. A general complexity approach is a deep philosophical engagement with complexity that is open, ontological, epistemologically modest and always ecologically and ethically embedded (Cilliers 2007; Morin 2008; Byrne and Callaghan 2014; Woermann 2016).

General complexity is, thus, a theory of systemic becomings and transformation and the endless novelty and force of creation. Complex systems arise, organise and operate in a field of ontogenetic forces in processes of open systemic creation, augmentation and transformations. Their organisation in dissipative structures and dynamic transversal consistencies generates a system that is constitutively organisationally open: both simultaneously disordered and ordered; both simultaneously dependent and autonomous from their environment; both simultaneously an inclusive systemic identity and an exclusive systemic identity (Morin 2007, 2008; Woermann 2016). Differences in complex systems do not cancel out and remain generative in a play of intensities across and beyond the complex system, with the complex system held together by the same way it falls apart: waves of creativity and waves of destruction, continuously pulsing with transformation.

Further, general complexity theory is transdisciplinary in scope, breaking down divisions between contemporary social sciences, humanities and its scientific worldview. It opens up a world where everything is processes and becomings, of ceaseless creativity and ever-increasing complexity of the world and life and of transformation. The very broad range of systems understood to be complex are all characterised by interconnectedness, systemic properties, instabilities and non-linearities, unpredictability, porous boundaries, some element of bottom-up organisation and rapid innovations.

The crux of Morin's distinction between restricted and general complexity, and a point that is just as important to mainstream complexity theory, is the relation between the conceptualisation of complexity and the modern scientific paradigm. The modern scientific paradigm is, of course, that of Newton, Descartes, Bacon et al., of a mechanistic universe, operating on timeless universal laws, with properties of essentialism and linearity. The knowledge paradigm to this mechanistic world is an analytical and reductivist, in which a thing can be understood in terms of breaking it down into its isolatable elements, and that knowing a thing entailed simplification, idealisations, standardisations and rationalisations. Contemporary complexity theory has come into existence, in its diverse variants, foundationally in the absolute recognition that the paradigm of modern science is fundamentally unable to explain or conceptualise the operation of complex systems. The operation of complexity in complex systems is the opposite of a mechanical world and reductionism (Capra and Mattei 2015). The post-reductionist complexity scientific approach is, thus, 'not that the law focused Newtonian science is wrong but rather that it is limited in its rightness' (Byrne and Callaghan 2014: 19).

There have to date been three sustained takes on developing a philosophically informed, and ontology heavy, general complexity: Morin's philosophy of General Systems Theory (Morin 2007, 2008; see also Cilliers 2007; Woermann 2016 for a poststructuralist development of Morin's theory), a Critical Realist informed ontology of complexity, exemplified by Byrne and Callaghan (2014) and the Deleuzian ontology of complexity, now taken up in the work of Delanda (2000, 2006, 2013, 2016), Massumi (1992) and Stengers (2000) (see Deleuze and Guattari 2017, 1986, 2004, 1994). Although all were concerned that complexity theory should develop as some sort of all-encompassing ontology of complex systems, there are various and sometimes important differences, between the three philosophical takes. Suffice it to remark here that the Morin/poststructuralist take tends towards the development of a phenomenological experience of the world and to ethical commitments, while the Critical Realist tends towards the development of concerns of agency, social structure and the development of applied social complexity research methodologies. The Deleuzian-inspired take tends towards the development of concerns of ecology and ethics, a social ontology of lines of flight and transformational becomings.

What is significant for this work is the conceptualisation of social systems as complex systems: Morin extended general complexity into social systems and arrangements and Byrne and Callaghan extended general complexity into social sciences, along with Chesters and Ward, in their complexity theory consideration of social movements (Chesters and Walsh 2007). However, the most sustained extension of complexity theory into the social field has been the assemblage theory of Deleuze and Guattari (2017, 1986, 2004, 1994), which we explore in detail below. In these approaches, complex social systems are understood as emerging and self-organising on a nature-culture continuum (Massumi 2013: 165). There is also broad agreement that the manner in which complexity organises and operates in complex physical and biological systems is also how complexity organises and operates in social systems. Indeed, it is made clear across the complexity theory literature approaches to social systems and social institutions that such systems are necessarily conceptualised as ecological and socio-ecological systems. Furthermore, social complexity is similarly beginning to find traction in legal studies (Ruhl 1996a, 1996b; Ruhl and Ruhl 1996; Murray 2008; Murray et al. 2018). As such, legal systems are increasingly understood as complex systemic social institutions, exhibiting characteristic complexity of far-from-equilibrium, self-organisation, emergence and edge-of-chaos critical dissipative creativity.

6.4 Deleuze and Guattari's Affective Assemblage Theory

Deleuze and Guattari's affective assemblage theory is the coming together of Deleuzian affective philosophy of incorporeal materialism, with ideas from philosophical general complexity. This work translates the scientific concepts of complexity science into theoretical concepts, with a direct focus on the social field and social institutions. The theory was developed in the joint work of Deleuze and Guattari through a series of books *Anti-Oedipus* (2017), *Kafka: Towards a Minor Literature* (1986), *A Thousand Plateaus* (2004), and *What Is Philosophy?* (1994). It was in the little book of *Kafka: Towards a Minor Literature* that Deleuze and Guattari first came to synthesise the affective field theory of Deleuze (see *Spinoza: A Practical Philosophy* (1988a), *Spinoza: Expressionism in Philosophy* (1992), *Bergsonism* (1991), *Difference and Repetition* (1994) and *Logic of Sense* (1990)) with their prescient appreciation and understanding of the emerging theory of complex systems. In the last chapter 'What is an Assemblage?', the novels of Kafka are considered as an exemplary affective assemblage and hence the key features of an assemblage are set out. *A Thousand Plateaus* (2004) substantially develops affective assemblage theory through linking a synthetic and integrative theory of intensive incorporeal materialistic ontology to a social metaphysics of social organisation and social operations. In this book, the theory of affective assemblages and a concept of affect comes to occupy the place of what *Anti-Oedipus* termed desiring production, and the concept of assemblaging forms the framework for the creation, investment and dynamics of social fields. The emphasis on embodied affect over desiring production reflects the much stronger influence of Spinoza in *A Thousand Plateaus* (Deleuze and Guattari 2004).

What Is Philosophy? (1994) returned to affective social assemblage theory in a chapter on the geophilosophy of territories and the assemblage processes of territorialisation, deterritorialisation and reterritorialisation. This publication revisited the Deleuze and Guattari concept of planes, and aligned a plane of organisation with conventional science, a plane of composition with art practices and a plane of immanence with a philosophy of concepts (Deleuze and Guattari 2004: 85–113). Thus, this affective social assemblage theory—developed across the Deleuze and Guattari collaboration—conceptualises social systems and social institutions in an intensive social field of social ontogenesis, but with a new set of investigative conceptual tools.

6.4.1 *Social Assemblages*

In this philosophical framework, assemblages emerge as dynamically complex organisation amongst bodies and affects that comprise an intensive assembly of the corporeal and incorporeal, in open and continuous movement. This process of the assembly of diverse bodies and affects is the vitality of matter that operates in immanent self-organisation amongst the flows of bodies and affects, producing emergent affective assemblages nested in emergent affective assemblages.

Hence, social assemblages come into being through complex self-organisation and can be understood as the co-existence and relay between the intensive and the actual register. As a complex system, they comprise multifarious elements, including: spatio-temporalities, spaces and durations, vibrant multidimensional flows, materialities, affects and affective bodies and dynamic interconnections and interactions amongst heterogeneities. In addition, there is the intensive assembling of the corporeal and incorporeal, the forming of social and ecological heterogeneities and a semiotic regime and a material regime in reciprocal presupposition. We can also see a heterogeneous coming together of qualities of things, that which inheres in substance and predicates, what things do and have done to them, the manner of things existing with each other, their causal interactions and the capacity of things to be transformed both in extension and thought. Assemblages emerge from the relations of things that affect and link things, the inherence of an excess, the conditions under which things change, the becomings of things both material and ideal and the conditions under which things can be thought and spoken.

6.4.2 Semiotic and Material Regimes

A social assemblage will comprise both a semiotic and material regime. The former emerges from heterogeneous forms of expression and sayabilities (Deleuze 1988: 10)—in speaking, language, statements and discourses—bringing forth formalised or finalised functions in the discursive formation of statements (Deleuze 1988: 65). We should recognise these emergence and heterogenous forms of expression and sayabilities in semiotics as precisely the logic of sense explore in the previous chapter. However, in a social assemblage, there is never a pure expression of sensation and sense, rather there is a regime of coding forms of expression and sense, of formalised or finalised functions that are revealed by statements, speaking and sayabilities (Deleuze 1988: 65). Not only are there heterogeneous forms of expression in the discursive formations, but there is also the important development of the regimes of statements (Deleuze 1988: 10).

In contrast, the material regime emerges from heterogeneous forms of content and visibilities (Deleuze 1988: 10)—in light, seeing, scenes, social institutions and the material-built environment—bringing forth formed substances revealed by the visibility of a formed materiality (Deleuze 1988: 10). As such, it flows from affective atmospheres. Hence, the material regime is the non-discursive formation of institutions. It is a material regime of stratification and formed content of bodies, buildings, streets and spaces. The material register is the form of content of formal substances that are revealed by visibility and seeing (Deleuze 1988: 65). It is the non-discursive formations of heterogeneous forms of content and institutions (Deleuze 1988: 10).

Both the semiotic and material regimes self-organise and code/stratify in a reciprocal presupposition of perpetual disequilibrium, churning on an emerging transversal consistency and dissipative structure. Coding and stratification can be understood as lines of capture of affective assemblages by social assemblages, as things become complicated as well as complex, and there is the formalisation of the social in the coding and stratification of speaking and seeing, light and language and constituting social knowledge.

Deleuze and Guattari specify a range of social assemblage semiotic regimes, and different organisations of the interconnection and interactions of the semiotic and material regimes. There are pre-signifying semiotic regimes, signifying semiotic regimes, post-signifying semiotic regimes and counter-signifying semiotic regimes (Deleuze and Guattari 2004). Some semiotic regimes assume a counter-signifying semiotic regime of affects that is openly interconnected and interacting with the material regime, and both openly expressively intermingle and change. However, some semiotic regimes, such as signifying regimes, seek to autopoetically exclude any reciprocal presupposition with a material regime, in a closed self-referential semiotic. Such semiotic regimes seek to draw a self-contained linguistic and discursive plane of organisation, imposing dominant transcendent signifying forms of matter rendered passive and all social assemblage affective intensity cancelled out.[4]

6.4.3 *Territorialisation, Deterritorialisation and Reterritorialisation*

As we explained in Chap. 2, while social assemblages come into being through process of self-organisation and emergence, they undergo profound processes of territorialisation.[5] They create and set their own territory, and this relates to the concept of the refrain. Social assemblages emerge in a refrain, (Deleuze and Guattari 1994: 185) which is a diagram and expressionism as the ground of territorialisation (Deleuze and Guattari 1994: 183). Through these processes of territorialisation, social assemblages organise their own space that they create their territory into. This social space can be smooth or striated, with smooth space facilitating free flowing affective production, while striated space constrains the very possibilities for affective production and the very nature of the territory that can be constructed (Deleuze and Guattari 1994: 185). Concomitantly, territories codify affective bodies and social flows. As such, social assemblages are always socio-ecological systems; they constitutively territorialise the vitality of matter, the affective capacities of bodies and potentials for becoming and transformation. Hence, they are the social production of sense and the social production of truth.

Different social assemblages draw different territories. Social assemblages may draw a territory that is sparse and fluid, relatively mobile and of potentially fleeting duration (e.g. a performance art assemblage, a circus assemblage). Another assemblage draws a territory, whether large or small, deeply entrenched geographically and very long-term duration, with very clear inside/outside territorial boundaries. The idea of a territory brings with it the geography, spatio-temporal scale and reach of the social assemblage. It also brings with it an idea of the centrality of expressive markings that create and constitute the assemblage territory—its colours, sounds, scents, arranged objects and the signs by which a territory is seen and sensed. The territory is the interaction of social functions and social expressive markers and the assemblage's affective atmosphere. It is also the matters of a social assemblage, its land, its characteristic material objects and all its built environment and the bodies that encounter each other in these enclosed spaces and the signs they emit there. The concept of a social assemblage's territory further brings a sense of a body being put in place, even some sense of security or home and a sense and truth of leaving of a territory and the coming back to a territory, a rhythm of leaving and returning. The concept also includes at its limits, some idea of leaving a territory for good, of leaving the social assemblage and never going home again. Thus a territory might be a house and all that is said and goes on there, a street and all that occupies that street and what is said and goes on there, or a social institution in so far as it occupies land and buildings, assembled bodies and all that is said and done by that institution and stretches into neighbouring social fields.

However, in Deleuze and Guattari's theory of social assemblages, territorialisation does not once and for all code and stratify a fixed territory. Social assemblages are run through with forces and processes of deterritorialisation. Deterritorialisation is a process of smoothing striated space, decoding affective bodies and social flows, de-subjectification and de-stratifying territory.[6] For Deleuze and Guattari deterritorialisation is an inevitable feature of territorialisation. Even if a social assemblage establishes a territory that is closed, and codes and stratifies the bodies and social flows, the vitality of matter installs forces of ceaseless creation and change in every social assemblage. In social assemblages, deterritorialisation manifests itself as lines of flight, freeing bodies from restrictions and boundaries of control, and unleashing new social experimentation and increased capacities for affect and becomings.[7] Deterritorialisation/lines of flight are points of creativity and change and the creative and generative forces of the social assemblage and its capacities for entering into new relations and transformations. Not all deterritorialisations are entirely the affirmation of affective capacity and life. There can be destroying deterritorialisation of black holes, and those such as the deterritorialisation of drug addiction. However, for Deleuze and Guattari, deterritorialisation is the immanent social force that makes escapes from social capture and control, and the exploration of affective potentials to become in new ways of affirming life.

For Deleuze and Guattari the forces of social assemblaging do not allow the free escape and liberation of deterritorialisation. Deterritorialisation is followed by processes of reterritorialisation. Social space is restriated, affective bodies and social flows are recoded, and territorial destratifications restratified. It is not that the operations of reterritorialisation exactly undo the operation of deterritorialisation. The restriation, recoding and restratification may even be substantially different to the prior striation, coding and strata, perhaps allowing greater scope for affective production. However, Deleuze and Guattari suggest that a deterritorialisation that is not recuperated in some way by reterritorialisation will be rare. Thus, rather than being absolute, deterritorialisation will be relative. Accordingly, in Deleuze and Guattari's account of social assemblage there is to be expected a constant and never-ending relay in complex social assemblages of processes of territorialisation, deterritorialisation and reterritorialisation.[8]

6.4.4 *Transversal Consistencies of Social Assemblages*

A crucial feature of complex social assemblages is precisely that they hold together in intensity and immanence that Deleuze and Guattari termed as transversal consistency (Deleuze and Guattari 2004). Within the context of the discussion of complex ontogenesis, transversal consistency can be understood as dissipative structure and self-organised criticality. In the differential force relations of the intensive social field, the emergence of the dissipative structure and self-organising criticality creates and holds together the social assemblage. Transversal consistency can be understood as differential attunements (Massumi 2013: 128) and its emergence is processual and relational, forming a dynamic consistency amongst the affects as embodied connections. If the dissipative structure organising the social assemblage is to lose its transversal consistency, then there is the collapse of the social assemblage into dynamically unrelated actual parts.

We can now link this to the two social planes explored in the previous chapter. As we noted, there is a plane of composition of sensations, intensities, bodies, affects, affective atmospheres, self-organisation, emergence, becomings and transformations of the decoded and deterritorialised. In contrast, the plane of organisation comprises the territorialised and reterritorialised strata and codings (Deleuze and Guattari 1994: 185).

6.4.5 *Social Assemblages and Social Regimes*

Social assemblages may be schools, hospitals and corporations, as well as informal social associations. They can also be very large scale. The state is the classic example of a social assemblage of capture. Foucault's governance of the nineteenth century is a social assemblage of discipline, and the global capitalism of the late twentieth and early twenty first centuries a social assemblage of control. Social assemblages emerge to organise affective assemblages to striate the social space, to code the social bodies and to territorialise all the social bodies, flows and milieus (Deleuze and Guattari 2004).

It is, however, important to distinguish social assemblages and social *regimes*. A social regime constructs codes for bodies and social flows, capturing and controlling bodies' affects and capacities to affect and be affected. It brings together seeing and speaking, statements and scenes, light and language, but operates at once to codify and stratify the intensive social field into the actual social field and its actual meanings and actual things. Hence, social regimes are assemblages of capture, with affective assemblages caught up in social assemblages. For Deleuze and Guattari's theory of social assemblages, there is always the capture, containment, control and even prohibition of affective assemblages in social regimes (Deleuze and Guattari 2004 'Apparatus of Capture').

6.4.6 *The Field of Affective Social Assemblages*

An affective social assemblage forms out of a field and also comes to occupy that field, and this is the same field as the intensive field that was explored in Chap. 2, but in its social formation. This field is neither benevolent nor law like. Rather, it is a field of infinite complexity in chaos, comprising an intensive field of forces of matter movement, the social field of the incorporeals and the inherence of forms of order in the flows of processes and objects. It is in perpetual disequilibrium, on a nature-culture continuum (organic, nonorganic and social) and, as such, necessarily ecological, with the incorporeal potentialisation of social matters and materials of social systems forming the intensive social milieus. The intensive social milieus are the intensive social regime of heterogeneities between unformed semiotic fragments and unformed material fragments. These are the intensive sites of composition of forces, of social sensations, social affects, social bodies and social affects of becomings, along with material elements, such as fragments of built environment, ecological fragments (i.e. weather and food chains), partial visibilities, partial sayabilities, in intensive reciprocal presupposition.

To explain this further, the social field can be conceptualised as an affective assemblage of heterogeneities between unformed semiotic and material flows in an intensive coming together. It is a field of social becomings, social events and bifurcations, social self-organisation of affects, of being ecologically-socially, being affected and affecting and a field of social transformations. As such, it is a field of social order-out of chaos, self-organisation, emergence, dissipative structures and self-organising criticality. This is a social field of social forces and power and the capture of social forces by social power (Deleuze 1988). Significantly, however, this social power is not a power over things, but capacities to act in particular ways, either at the level of corporeal behaviour and/or at the level of mental elaboration (Grosz 2017: 83).

In developing this ontogenetic concept of the intensive social field, Deleuze and Guattari are bringing forward the ontology of Deleuze's incorporeal materialism and connecting it to their newly formed ontology of complexity. Thus, in affective social assemblage theory the intensive social field is the ontogenetic social field and a social problem field. As in the incorporeal materialist ontology of Deleuze and the scientific methodology of complexity science and general complexity theory, the social field is mappable in terms in terms of high dimensionality manifolds and a dynamic distribution of singularities and attractors. Such a way of thinking about complex assemblages allows us to think through a complex assemblage's attractors, bifurcation points, events, affects and being affected, emergence, dissipative structures, self-organising criticality, becomings and transformation. In complex social assemblage theory thinking about social systems and social institutions in terms of high dimensionality manifolds and distribution of attractors and singularities is necessarily intuitive and experimental, affective and beyond representation. This social assemblage theory centres on the development of a cartographic project of 'mapping complex, embodied, relational, spatial, affective energies' across the social field (Ringrose 2011: 599). The theory maps a social field of flows and attachments that are embodied, intensely affective and complexly assembled. It is a practice of attentiveness to mapping micro political relations of affective assemblages and to mapping the power relations amongst assembled bodies in social assemblages.

6.5 Conclusion: The Courtroom as an Affective Assemblage

A courtroom is ultimately a matter of the pragmatic, deployment and marshalling of affects, sense-making and the production of emergent truths. The courtroom is a space of theatre and dramaturgy, and a plane of composition encompassing a material-semiotic counter-signifying regime of non-representational drama, with complex territories, deterritorialising lines of flight and multiple reterritorialisations. The courtroom as affective social assemblage encompasses the physical, architectural, the courtroom itself and wider court building the streets abutting the court building, along with all the bodies that enter into these spaces (the bodies of judges, of barristers, court officials, defendants, complainants, witnesses, police officers, family members, solicitors and reporters) and all the expressive materials that pass between these bodies and across these spaces (words, noises, looks, gazes, smells and clothing). Barristers are the directors of courtroom drama—they are those who know how to marshal affects in the affective assemblage of actors and stage. The director calls forth the affective assemblage/affective emissions of the actors and sets affects into inter-relations with other produced affects across the stage: connecting affects in duration, eliciting speeds and slownesses across the action, coordinating the affects that lessen affects and the stronger affects that enter into battle and overpower the previous overpowering affect. Whilst the play unfolds, the affects and intensities pile up, fates invoked but uncertain, speeding to the denouement. All the intensities cancel out, what has been transpiring has transpired, the intensive is now actual, the affects are now just feelings of a past feeling, an account of what went on, a representation of a scenario.

Notes

1. Drawing upon the empirical data, as well as law and policy documents, we identify and examine the attractors within the rape courtroom assemblage in considerable detail in Chaps. 2, 3 and 4. For further detail, see endnote 4 in Chap. 5. An analysis of the data enables us to a develop phase space mapping of various bifurcation points that operate within a rape trial. Examples include conviction rates (Sect. 2.3), consent (Sect. 3.2.1), the use of special measures (Sect. 4.3) and changing cross-examination techniques (Sect. 4.5).
2. The aim of the data chapters is to engage in a mapping process in order to render perceptible the operation of the intensive incorporeals within the rape courtroom affective assemblage. This, we argue, engenders a deeper understanding of the trial process.
3. The phenomena of self-organisation, emergence and non-linearity within the rape courtroom assemblage, and barristers' understandings of such, can be seen in relation to various factors, as highlighted in Chap. 5 endnote 3.
4. The semiotic regime of the courtroom affective assemblage is explored in detail in Chap. 3 and the material in Chap. 4. However, throughout we highlight how the two regimes are inextricably intertwined. For barristers, the role of discourse and expression in a trial is to produce affects in juries, and significant attention is given to the ability of the body to affect and be affected. This in turn fundamentally influenced their reception of various reforms and measures.
5. We focus specifically on the rape courtroom territory in Chap. 4. See in particular Sect. 4.2, which explores barristers' perspectives regarding the adoption of the achieving best evidence video.
6. In Chap. 3, we explore barristers' preference for smooth over striated spaces, as this enables the marshalling of affects, self-organisation, emergence and the drawing of a plane of composition. We highlight how substantive law can be seen as a form of over-coding which could frequently sit in tension with barristers' techniques of affect. See in particular Sects. 3.2.1, 3.2.2, 3.2.3 and 3.2.4. This in turn could lead to a decoding, and we highlight the rejection of the presumptions relating to consent (s. 75 and s. 76 *Sexual Offences Act 2003*) as a significant example of such. In general, over-coding was not perceived by advocates to be the solution to the challenges arising from rape cases.
7. The empirical data indicates the presence of numerous lines of flight, some fleeting, other more sustained. See for example the discussion relating to conviction rates (Sect. 2.3); the reformulated mens rea test, which requires belief in consent to be reasonable (Sect. 3.2.2); the adoption of the mistaken assumption directions (Sect. 3.3); the use of special measures (Sect. 4.3);

changing cross-examination techniques (Sect. 4.5); and unexpected complainant courtroom performances (Sect. 4.6). The key argument is that these lines of flight provide an opportunity for change.

8. Processes of relative deterritorialisation and reterritorialisation could be seen to flow throughout the rape courtroom assemblage and the practice of barristers. See for example the discussions in relation to mens rea (Sect. 3.2.2); the mistaken assumptions directions (Sect. 3.3.1); the use of special measures (Sects. 4.2 and 4.3); changing cross-examination practices (Sect. 4.5); and unexpected and challenging complainant performances (Sect. 4.6).

References

Bak, P. (1996). *How Nature Works: The Science of Self-Organised Criticality.* New York: Copernicus.

Bak, P., Ting, C., & Wiesenfeld, K. (1987). Self-Organising Criticality. *Physical Review of Letters, 59*(4), 381–384.

Byrne, D., & Callaghan, G. (2014). *Complexity Theory and the Social Sciences.* Abingdon: Routledge.

Capra, F. (2014). *The Systems View of Life: A Unifying Vision.* Cambridge: Cambridge University Press.

Capra, F., and Mattie, U. (2015). *The Ecology of Law: Towards a Legal System in Tune with Nature and Community.* Oakland CA: Berrett-Koehler.

Chesters, G., & Walsh, I. (2007). *Complexity and Social Movements: Multitudes at the Edge of Chaos.* Abingdon: Routledge.

Cilliers, P. (2007). *Thinking Complexity: Complexity and Philosophy.* London: ISCE Publishing.

Colander, D., & Kupers, R. (2014). *Complexity and the Art of Public Policy.* Princeton: Princeton University Press.

Coveney, P., & Highfield, R. (1995). *Frontiers of Complexity: The Search for Order in a Chaotic World.* London: Faber and Faber.

Delanda, M. (2000). *A Thousand Years of Nonlinear History.* New York: Zone Books.

Delanda, M. (2006). *A New Philosophy of Society: Assemblage Theory and Social Complexity.* London: Continuum.

Delanda, M. (2013). *Intensive Science, Virtual Philosophy.* London: Bloomsbury.

Delanda, M. (2016). *Assemblage Theory.* Edinburgh: Edinburgh University Press.

Deleuze, G. (1988). *Foucault.* London: Continuum.

Deleuze, G., & Guattari, F. (1986). *Kafka: Toward a Minor Literature.* Minneapolis: University of Minneapolis Press.

Deleuze, G., & Guattari, F. (1994). *What Is Philosophy?* London: Verso.

Deleuze, G., & Guattari, F. (2004). *A Thousand Plateaus.* London: Continuum.

Deleuze, G., & Guattari, F. (2017). *Anti-Oedipus.* London: Bloomsbury.

Gleick, J. (1987). *Chaos: Making a New Science*. London: Vintage.

Grosz, E. (2017). *The Incorporeal: Ontology, Ethics, and the Limits of Materialism*. New York: Columbia University Press.

Guattari, F. (2000). *The Three Ecologies*. London: Athlone Press.

Holland, J. (1999). *Emergence: From Chaos to Order*. Oxford: Oxford University Press.

Kauffman, S. (1995). *At Home in the Universe: The Search for Laws of Self-Organisation and Complexity*. Oxford: Oxford University Press.

Kauffman, S. (2000). *Investigations*. Oxford: Oxford University Press.

Kauffman, S. (2008). *Reinventing the Sacred*. New York: Basic Books.

Lorenz, E. (1993). *The Essence of Chaos*. Seattle: Washington University Press.

Massumi, B. (1992). *A User's Guide to Capitalism and Schizophrenia: Deviations from Deleuze and Guattari*. Massachusetts: The MIT Press.

Massumi, B. (2013). *Semblance and Event: Activist Philosophy and Occurrent Acts*. Massachusetts: MIT Press.

Morin, E. (2007). Restricted Complexity, General Complexity. In C. Aerts & B. Edmonds (Eds.), *Worldviews, Science and Us: Philosophy and Complexity* (pp. 5–29). New Jersey: World Scientific.

Morin, E. (2008). *On Complexity*. London: Hampton Press.

Murray, J. (2008). Complexity Theory and Socio-Legal Studies. *Liverpool Law Review, 29*(2), 227–246.

Murray, J., Webb, T., & Wheatley, S. (Eds.). (2018). *Law's Complexity: Mapping an Emergent Jurisprudence*. Abingdon: Routledge.

Prigogine, I., & Stengers, I. (1989). *Order Out of Chaos*. London: Bantom Double Day.

Ringrose, J. (2011). Beyond Discourse? Using Deleuze and Guattari's Schizoanalysis to Explore Affective Assemblages, Heterosecually Striated Space, and Lines of Flight Online and at School. *Educational Philosophy and Theory, 43*(6), 598–618.

Ruhl, J. B. (1996a). Complexity Theory as a Paradigm for the Dynamic Law-and-Society System: A Wake-up Call for the Legal Reductionism and the Modern Administrative State. *Duke Law Journal, 45*(5), 849–928.

Ruhl, J. B. (1996b). The Fitness of Law: Using Complexity Theory to Describe the Evolution of Law and Society and Its Practical Meaning for Democracy. *Vanderbilt Law Review, 49*, 1406–1492.

Ruhl, J. B., & Ruhl, H. (1996). The Arrow of Law in Modern Administrative States: Using Complexity Theory to Reveal the Diminishing Returns and Increasing Risks the Burgeoning of Law Poses to Society. *UC Davis Law Review, 30*, 405–482.

Scheffer, M. (2009). *Critical Transitions in Nature and Society*. Princeton: Princeton University Press.

Stengers, I. (2000). *The Invention of Modern Science*. Minneapolis: University of Minnesota.
Waldrop, M. (1992). *Complexity: The Emerging Science at the Edge of Order and Chaos*. London: Simon and Schuster.
Woermann, M. (2016). *Bridging Complexity and Post-Structuralism: Insights and Implications*. Berne: Springer.

CHAPTER 7

Conclusion: Techniques of Affect and Adaptive Management

Abstract The original argument made in this book is that the courtroom in rape cases is not well understood representationally or in terms of a plane of organisation. Rather, our unique position is that the courtroom and barristers' practices and views are best understood in terms of an affective assemblage and an intensive self-organising plane of composition. In conclusion, we contemplate what this reconceptualisation means for practitioners, legislators and policymakers. This involves revisiting and further expounding the practice of 'techniques of affect' and introducing the concept of 'adaptive management'. We argue that the theoretical and speculative pragmatic approach adopted enables us to better inform legislators and policymakers of how practitioners really engage with policy initiatives and develop a common language for communicating with these three audiences in the avoidance of implementation gaps.

Keywords Techniques of affect • Practices of intensification • Adaptive management • Iterative processes • Feedback loops • Bridging organisations

The argument made in this book is that orthodox frameworks of representational thinking and the plane of organisation are inadequate to

A. Carline et al., *Rape and the Criminal Trial*, Palgrave Socio-Legal Studies, https://doi.org/10.1007/978-3-030-38684-9_7

understand the courtroom in rape cases. Rather, our unique position is that the courtroom and barristers' practices and views are best theorised in terms of an affective assemblage and an intensive self-organising plane of composition. We have argued that the rape courtroom is, ultimately, a matter of deploying and marshalling affects, sense-making and the production of emergent truths and that barristers intuitively understand and work the intensive ontological regime. Our key argument follows from our novel theoretical and methodological approach, which draws together Deleuzian new materialism and affect theory in order to develop new insights into criminal justice responses to rape. We have highlighted that the criminal courtroom has a double existence, operating on two different ontological registers: the intensive and the actual. It is the former that is critical to understanding what drives advocates' practices and the implementation (or otherwise) of law and policy reforms. Adopting this approach enables us to better inform legislators and policymakers of how practitioners really engage with policy initiatives and develop a common language for communicating with these audiences in the avoidance of implementation gaps. Based on these arguments, we encourage a broader application of the theoretical and methodology approach we have presented, and as such call for a crucial and essential re-orientation of the understanding of criminal justice, criminology and legal studies. In this conclusion, we consider further what the arguments laid out in this book mean for practitioners, legislators and policymakers by revisiting 'techniques of affect' and introducing the concept to 'adaptive management' (Ruhl and Fischman 2010).

7.1 Techniques of Affect: Participating in the Intensive

As we have explored, in Deleuze's account, in the plane of composition, participation and intervention must proceed by very different techniques to those in an actual plane of organisation. As demonstrated, an understanding of an incorporeal materialist ontology of affect can provide a novel way of understanding and working with affective assemblages such as criminal courtrooms. As we have outlined, these pragmatic insights are termed *techniques of affect* and composing a plane of composition (Deleuze 1988, 1990, 1991, 1992, 1994; Massumi 2002, 2013, 2015; Manning and Massumi 2014), which comprises the development of speculative and new practices of mapping, organising, operating and evaluating intensive social fields and affective assemblages and for calling forth life-affirming lines of flight. These techniques of affect correspond with what Deleuze theorises as a theatre of repetition, in contrast to a theatre of representation. The drama of the theatre of repetition is that of working with sensations, intensive bodies, affects, affective atmospheres and planes of composition (Deleuze 1990, 1994).

Participating and intervening in an affective assemblage, such as the criminal courtroom, begins with an exploration of its problem field, phase space and the distribution of singularities and attractors. This is a matter of 'determining problems and realising in them our power of creation and decision' (Deleuze 1994: 352). It also involves mapping the assemblage's semiotic and material regimes and the relations between the two. Throughout this book, we have engaged in that process. We have explored the problem field of the intensive courtroom, mapped the key attractors and singularities and investigated affect-events and the intensive incorporeal forces and relationships amongst the heterogeneous bodies. We have also examined processes of de/re/territorialisations. Having done so, we have rendered the intensive—that which is imperceptible—perceptible and this rendering is a key element of techniques of affect. Indeed, bringing to light the intensive ontological regime of the system is to make 'dimensions of experience that do not appear appear' (Massumi 2013: 24) and involves engaging in 'practices of intensification'. In developing this approach, Deleuze and Guattari turn to Peguy's account of two ways of exploring events:

> One consists in going over the course of the event, in recording its effectuation in history, its conditioning and deterioration in history. But the other consists in reassembling the event, installing oneself in it as in a becoming, becoming young again and ageing in it, both at the same time, going through all its components or singularities. (Deleuze and Guattari 1994: 111)

Hence, practices of intensification involve installing oneself in the problematic and the intensive event and opening oneself to the intensive register. This is to practice 'technique that takes as its "object" process itself, a speculative pragmatic production of orientated events of change … techniques dedicated to ontogenesis itself' (Massumi 2013: 14). Thus, to engage in practices of intensification is to orientate oneself towards the intensive, become sensitive to it and in so doing, see the dynamics of the world beyond the extensive plane of organisation.

Throughout a trial, we maintain that barristers are engaged in practices of intensification and techniques of affect. They have an intuitive sense of the intensive and are concerned to precipitate, activate, assist, unleash, deploy and produce affects in the courtroom, as well as trigger bifurcations in bodies off existing attractors and singularities (i.e. move them from not guilty to guilty, or vice versa). Barristers intervene in the intensive in order 'to move bodies without objectively touching them' (Massumi 2013: 126). With their preference for smooth over striated spaces, we can see how they understand and tap into the emergent and self-organisational reality of the courtroom, which is to compose and draw a plane of composition (Massumi 2013).

Indeed, as we have demonstrated in the data, another key technique of affect is that of sense-making, which involves the exploration of intensive sense in the problem field of the affective assemblage. This opens up the discursive dimension of the material body and state of affairs—and the scope for the exploration of the operation of incorporeals in language—in order to make sense of the system. Further, through making sense of the system it is possible to move the task of techniques of affect towards the complex adventure of composing a plane of composition. This involves practicing techniques of affect at the level of both material and discursive systems and the dynamic interconnections of the two. Importantly, this expands the scope for practicing techniques of affect, as these are now practicable in language. Such techniques enable pre-personal and pre-individual singularities to speak out (Deleuze 1990). That is, to trigger, through words, intensive processes in material bodies and states of affairs. We can see this clearly through the importance barristers attached to courtroom expressions and the intermingling of the semiotic and material regimes. Discourse and language in the courtroom, for barristers, is fundamentally concerned with triggering, managing and marshalling affects.

Techniques of affect can also be understood as techniques for the 'production of the true'. They can be deployed to extract truth from bodies and situations. That is, in the battle between the semiotic and material forces, intensive sense, or the 'truth', can enter into language and discourse. Thus, courtroom utterances and performances, specifically those which are unexpected and disruptive—which barristers often identified as being compelling—can be viewed as extracting/expressing an emergent intensive sense and truth about that body's actual and intensive reality.

Hence, we can understand that such techniques encompass drawing out intensive affect—that which is beyond representation—in language, and the data indicates barristers regularly participated in such practices. However, it is important to emphasise that techniques of affect also include rendering perceptible and marshalling the intensive affects that belong to images, such as photographs, videos and the visual theatre of the courtroom. While the data suggests that techniques of affect in relation to images were secondary to those pertaining to language in barristers' practice, there is necessarily a co-compositional relationship between the two. Exploring the techniques of affect relating to images is an area which could potentially be developed much further (in terms of both research and practice), particularly regarding the visual aspect of the ABE interview, which is played in court.

Understanding that techniques of affect are a fundamental element of practice is pivotal to the generation of measures that will be effectively implemented and used by practitioners. This, however, is not to argue against the introduction of provisions which barristers perceive as dampening their ability to incite affects in the courtroom, such as the use of remote testimony. Rather, it is to recognise why barristers may be resistant to well-meaning measures and to highlight the importance of working with advocates to explore how technology can be utilised to enhance the transmission of affects. Indeed, barristers' preference for bottom-up and emergent developments, from those they consider to have an intensive sense of the system, is a crucial factor in the development and implementation of measures and reiterates the importance of legislatures and policymakers working with practitioners in the development of new approaches. Importantly, it is also possible to shift bodies on to new basins of attraction, or even onto a chaotic attractor. This requires mapping the courtroom's territories and stratifications, perceiving, following and capitalising upon deterritorialisations, destratifications and lines of flight and understanding the dominant forces of reterritorialisation. With incorporeal forces rendered perceptible, more targeted intensive interventions may be attempted in order to trigger specific intensive processes that can alter actual bodies and states of affairs. For example, in assisting barristers to move away from the use of rape myths and towards more ethical examination technique. Indeed, in engaging in techniques of affect, it is possible 'to make things happen without explicitly ordering the steps to be followed' (Massumi 2013: 126).

Overall, if it is possible to develop an understanding of the system, how that system operates—both intensively and actually—it becomes possible to know how to intervene and produce measures which will accord to the sense of that system. Hence, while we have seen that barristers have been keen to trigger and marshal the affective potential of courtroom expressions and performances, legislators and policy makers can likewise intervene and participate in the courtroom affective assemblage and its intensive incorporeal processes. It is possible for criminal courtroom actors (broadly conceived) to strategise and experiment in the intensive in order to engender more productive, impactful and potentially ethical ways of practicing.

7.1.1 Techniques of Affect as Artistic, Political and Ethical Practices

Following Massumi's development of Deleuze and Guattari's assemblage theory, techniques of affect, taken at their broadest, can become a practice that is aesthetic, political and ethical (Massumi 2013, 2015; Manning and Massumi 2014). In relation to the former, Deleuze and Guattari (1994) liken the plane of composition to the plane of artistry and as such, techniques of affect can be viewed as an aesthetical working with intensities and sensations. Hence, we can understand barristers' engagement with them as artistic practice, with it not being unusual to liken an advocate's courtroom performance to acting (Drew 2007). However, the key point here is that by participating in the intensive, barristers are involved in a form of non-representational drama. In addition, techniques of affect have political and ethical dimensions. This is because they involve evaluations of the potential of assembled bodies and intervention into the intensive field to induce transformations and generate new collective assemblages. As Massumi explains, they involve 'a technique of composing potentials of existence, inventing experiential styles, coaxing new forms of life to emerge' (2015: 54) and as such, can be referred to as relational participatory politics (Massumi 2015). Thus, we can situate barristers'—indeed all courtroom performances—as innately political. While this may not accord with orthodox notions of law and criminal justice, or with how advocates interpret their practice, in rape cases in particular, it is difficult, if impossible, to divorce politics from the courtroom dynamic (see Carline and Gunby 2017).

Finally, techniques of affect have an ethical dimension. This emanates from the underlying philosophical ethos of the Spinozian approach to affects, which is concerned with enhancing the capabilities of bodies. To ethically engage in these affects is to be concerned with lines of flight and to have an overriding commitment to the flourishing of intensive life. Techniques of affect, thus, involve evaluating affective assemblages with regard to their ability to enable potentialities to be released that can free the immanent creativity of life from capture (allowing for emergence and self-organisation). As Massumi argues: 'It is always a question of freeing life whenever it is imprisoned' (Deleuze and Guattari 1994: 171). Hence, techniques of affect and drawing a plane of composition involve an ethic of exploring what a body can do and calling forth the flourishing of affective communities (Massumi 2015). Of course, they can also be used in unethical and negative ways. Massumi explains how the far right have used affects of fear and hope to 'capture the imagination of a population and produce nationalist feelings and tendencies' (2015: 35). As our data has highlighted, they can, and continue to be used in problematic ways in courtrooms to incite performances that conform to stereotypical scripts that impact negatively upon complainants. However, when they are deployed ethically, they are an exemplary example of intensive social ontogenesis. They involve the machining (the marshalling and bringing together) of transversal consistencies, working with territories and lines of flight and ultimately evaluating the vitality of the assemblage. Thus, we can understand, and maintain a commitment to work towards, the court as an affective assemblage of processes that are cultural and political, aesthetic and political, pragmatic and speculative, philosophical, artistic, relational and ethical.

7.2 Adaptive Management: Managing and Regulating Complex Systems

In complementing our discussion of techniques of affect there is a burgeoning literature on adaptive management which provides further novel insight into how to manage and regulate complex systems, such as the criminal courtroom, in order to work towards improved implementation and practice (Ruhl 2008; Walker and Salt 2008; Helbing 2008, 2009; Chandler 2014). Adaptive management was initially conceived by C. S. Holling in 1978, emerging from his dissatisfaction with the assessment processes and models adopted by Environmental Impact Assessment (EIA) teams in relation to environmental ecosystems (Holling 1978;

Ruhl 2004, 2005; Garmestani and Benson 2013; Garmestani and Allen 2014; Cheffin et al. 2016). These one-off and predictive assessment practices were considered insufficient to enable suitably comprehensive analysis of the system. They neither provided opportunity for post-implementation or rolling testing to verify hypotheses and generate real-time knowledge of the impact of actions and regulations. This, in turn, precluded scientists from recommending and implementing further adjustments and improvements to the system.

Holling's argument was that impact assessment must be an incremental, ongoing, iterative and reflective process, involving interdisciplinary teams and permit ongoing adaption and change. As Karkkainen (2005–2006: 60) explains, in describing a more productive approach to assessment, and the management style that developed to support it, teams of scientists

> [c]onstruct integrative models based upon the best data and research available, identify gaps and uncertainties and generate testable hypotheses; working with managers, the scientists would design management interventions as scientific experiments to test their hypotheses and outcomes.

As this was a repetitive and rolling process, the results of the experiment's informed refinements to actions followed by the production of further 'testable hypotheses' (Karkkainen 2005–2006: 61). This enabled the generation of real-world understanding of the ecological system and how it responded to the various models and actions. This knowledge was then used to inform and improve the decisions and practices of managers (Karkkainen 2005–2006). Hence, adaptive management can be described as 'an iterative, incremental decision-making process built around a continuous process of monitoring the effects of decisions and adjusting decisions accordingly' (Ruhl 2005: 29).

Importantly, adaptive management is based upon complexity theory and is a processual management style that can deal with non-linearity, uncertainty and unpredictability within complex systems and assemblages. It is a multi-faceted operation which involves understanding complex systems, such as the courtroom, in terms of 'threshold for regime change' (i.e. moving a system from one regime to another) and involves exploring the phase space of the system, mapping its attractors and the shape of its basins of attraction. The approach calls for the adoption of highly flexible and discretionary management practices, data driven monitoring, measuring and mapping of the system and then measuring and mapping evaluation, intervention and modification practices. This involves adaptive planning and identifying regulatory goals, with iterative and evolving processes of regulation and management. The monitoring of specific variables, attributes and drivers is thus central to the approach and requires the constant collation and evaluation of data. Data on the dynamics of the system allows adaptive managers to map and model the interconnections between heterogeneous bodies and to allow for a better understanding of how the system operates. Through this mapping and modelling, it is possible to start to understand multiple state thresholds (where change may be possible), adaptive cycles and the relationships between the multi-levels of the system. By engaging in such mapping, it is possible to pinpoint moments in the system which are more open to intervention.

As the name indicates, adaptive management adapts. It is a style of management that responds to changing conditions through intervening in complex system dynamics, monitoring the consequences of the management intervention and then feeding that information back into the planning and implementation of the intervention. An adaptive management technique develops by learning the design of mechanisms for moving and triggering thresholds and basins of attraction and tapping into and harnessing systemic self-organisation/emergence. Thus, it is a form of management that itself adapts to the changing conditions and dynamics in the system. Accordingly, it is experimental and innovative, entailing interventions that are 'trial and error in uncertainty'. It is a procedural framework for learning about the system whilst that system is being managed, for integrating learning into management processes and progressively learning to make more effective management interventions.

As indicated, key to adaptive management is its adoption of a 'back-ended approach'. This is because it comprises ongoing and post-implementation monitoring, evaluation and refinement of the system, allowing for further experimentation and change. Adaptive management is thus continuous—continuous learning, experimentation, iterative feedback loops, innovations and adaptations (Garmestani and Benson 2013; Garmestani and Allen 2014). This enables a comprehensive understanding of how the system works, the impact of regulations and changes, the emergence of lines of flight, an appreciation of moments of non-linearity and self-organisation and the ability to experiment with different responses to system change.

The application of adaptive management approaches to the development of law and policy responses clearly seems opportune. Generating feedback and data on the operation of measures in practice (in real time) enables modifications to be instituted that can adapt the system in response to unanticipated consequences. Currently, orthodox legality tends to prioritise front-ended approaches. Assessments of how the regulation or action may impact upon the system are carried out either pre-implementation and/or through an initial (typically) small-scale evaluation of the system, for example, via the adoption of pilot projects. These tend to be one-off events that preclude sophisticated monitoring and mapping in real-time or system driven (bottom-up) approaches. As Ruhl explains, adaptive management 'allows agencies to learn about and respond to changing conditions at the "back end" rather than loading all decision making at the "front end", when the effects of decisions and of other changing conditions are not yet known' (2005: 1265). To put this differently, whereas the front-ended approach 'evaluates all rational considerations at once and then flips a toggle switch; the adaptive management approach twiddles the dial as information trickles in' (Ruhl and Fischman 2010: 424). There is no one-off significant reform and attendant evaluation that is assumed to bring about substantial change; rather, reform needs to be incremental, reflective and continually responsive to system data. At present, rape law reform and policy adopt a 'front-end' approach that fails to recognise the courtroom as an affective assemblage. Such an approach is inadequate for responding to the complex and dynamic reality of the rape courtroom assemblage—the reality of emergence, self-organisation and non-linearity and the dynamic interactions between heterogeneous affective bodies.

Ruhl (2005), in his work, explores the following eight steps of adaptive management which we believe can be applied to those who develop and implement legal and policy responses to rape. As developed by the Klamath River Basin management committee, these comprise:

> (1) definition of the problem, (2) determination of goals and objectives for management [or reform of] the … system, (3) determination of the … system baseline [i.e. how the system currently operates], (4) development of conceptual [reform and policy] models, (5) selection of future [reform] actions, (6) implementation of management [or reform] actions, (7) monitoring and []system response, and (8) evaluation of restoration [reform] efforts and proposals for remedial actions. (2005: 29)

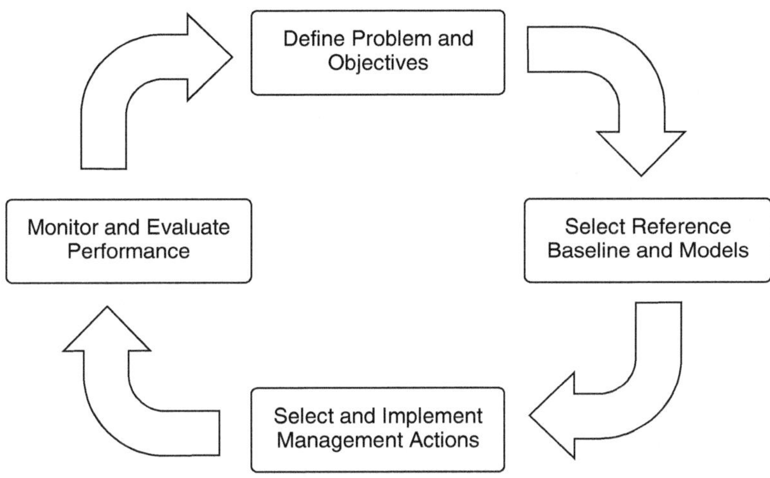

Fig. 7.1 Four core functions of adaptive management

As noted, it is important not to approach these eight stages in a linear fashion and to appreciate the continuous and iterative nature of the process. Ruhl (2005: 34), thus, suggests that the eight stages are best presented as the following four key functions (Fig. 7.1).

Undoubtedly, adaptive management is a considerable undertaking which will require significant resources in an already resource-poor system (Parliament 2017). However, at the same time, the pervasive nature of the rape law/policy implementation gap, the money already invested in (unsuccessful) efforts to increase convictions and decrease attrition and the lament that 'nothing much changes' (Cook 2011), indicates that a new approach is required. The constant 'review-go-round' (Jordan 2011) and production of numerous, detailed recommendations tend towards a top-down, front-ended approach which fails to take into account the working reality of the system and the complex, multi-level dynamics which comprise the courtroom in rape cases. At the same time, it is recognised that the adoption of adaptive management has proved difficult within the field of environmental and natural resources. As Karkkainen notes: '[w]hile some form of adaptive management is seen as axiomatic, even the most well-funded and technically sophisticated ecosystem management efforts are still struggling to integrative adaptive management principles' (2005–2006: 61). Accordingly, we recognise that full-scale adoption of the principles is unlikely; nevertheless, they can be drawn upon in order to move towards the adoption of more realistic and responsive reform endeavours. They also provide a unique framework for researchers to adopt (and test) who wish to explore the workings of the system and devise responses for addressing implementation failures.

As part of this, it is important to remain cognisant of barristers' misgivings regarding policy and reforms produced by those they perceived to lack a working knowledge and intensive sense of the system. The adoption of adaptive management goes some way to alleviate these concerns because the iterative feedback processes and continual evaluation should involve the adaptation of provisions based on the experiences of practitioners who have a working and intensive sense of the system. They will also potentially enable the identification and harnessing of more progressive lines of flight. However, in addition to this, and again drawing upon ecosystem literature, a further adaptive management concept and practice is that of 'bridging organisations' (see e.g. Garmestani et al. 2009). This comprises representatives from different scales/levels of the system, which could include, for example, policy makers, members of the bar and judiciary, police, witness and victim support groups, who oversee the adaptive management processes. Further, as Garmestani et al. explain, bridging organisations 'should act as mini think-tanks that facilitate communication between institutions, incubate new ideas for [system] management, and provide a forum for coming to agreements on contentious issues' (2009: 1053). By drawing upon principles of adaptive management and the role of bridging organisations it becomes possible to move towards the generation of bottom-up policy, which is reflective and responsive to the intensive reality of the courtroom.

References

Carline, A., & Gunby, C. (2017). Rape Politics, Policies and Practice: Exploring the Tensions and Unanticipated Consequences of Well-Intended Victim-Focused Measures. *The Howard Journal of Crime and Justice, 56*(1), 34–52.

Chandler, D. (2014). *Resilience: The Governance of Complexity.* Abingdon: Routledge.

Cheffin, B. C., Garmestani, A. S., Gunderson, L. H., Benson, M. H., Angeler, D. G., Arnold, C. A. A., Cosens, B., Craig, R. K., & Allen, C. R. (2016). Transformative Ecological Governance. *Annual Review of Environment and Resources, 41*, 399–432.

Cook, K. (2011). Rape Investigation and Prosecution: Stuck in the Mud? *Journal of Sexual Aggression, 17*(3), 250–262.
Deleuze, G. (1988). *Spinoza: Practical Philosophy*. San Francisco: City Lights.
Deleuze, G. (1990). *Logic of Sense*. London: Athlone Press.
Deleuze, G. (1991). *Bergsonism*. New York: Zone Books.
Deleuze, G. (1992). *Expressionism in Philosophy: Spinoza*. New York: Zone Books.
Deleuze, G. (1994). *Difference & Repetition*. London: Athlone Press.
Deleuze, G., & Guattari, F. (1994). *What Is Philosophy?* London: Verso.
Drew, S. K. (2007). Doing Justice. In S. K. Drew, E. D. Reed, M. Mills, & B. M. Gassaway (Eds.), *Dirty Work: The Social Construction of Taint* (pp. 11–32). Baylor University Press.
Garmestani, A. S., & Allen, C. (2014). *Social-Ecological Resilience and Law*. Columbia University Press.
Garmestani, A. S., & Benson, M. H. (2013). A Framework for Resilience Based Governance of Social-Ecological Systems. *Ecology & Society, 18*(1), 9–20.
Garmestani, A. S., Allen, C. R., & Cabezas, H. (2009). Panarchy, Adaptive Management and Governance: Policy Options for Building Resilience. *Nebraska Law Review, 87*(4), 1036–1054.
Helbing, D. (2008). *Managing Complexity: Insights, Concepts, Applications*. London: Springer.
Helbing, D. (2009). Managing Complexity in Socio-Economic Systems. *European Review, 17*, 423–438.
Holling, C. S. (1978). *Adaptive Environmental Assessment and Management*. Caldwell, NJ: Blackburn Press.
Jordan, J. (2011). Here We Go Round the Review-Go-Round: Rape Investigation and Prosecution – Are Things Getting Worse not Better? *Journal of Sexual Aggression, 17*(3), 234–249.
Karkkainen, B. C. (2005–2006). Panarchy and Adaptive Change: Around the Loop and Back Again. *Minnesota Journal of Law, Science Technology, 7*, 59–78.
Manning, E., & Massumi, B. (2014). *Thought in the Act: Passages in the Ecology of Experience*. Minneapolis: University of Minnesota Press.
Massumi, B. (2002). *Parables for the Virtual: Movement, Affect, Sensation*. Durham: Duke University Press.
Massumi, B. (2013). *Semblance and Event: Activist Philosophy and the Occurrent Arts*. Massachusetts: MIT Press.
Massumi, B. (2015). *Politics of Affect*. Cambridge: Polity.
Parliament. (2017). *Ministry of Justice Expenditure: Written Question – 1125414*. Retrieved September 6, 2019, from www.parliament.uk/business/publications/written-questions-answers-statements/written-question/Commons/2017-11-13/112641/.
Ruhl, J. B. (2004). Taking Adaptive Management Seriously: A Case Study of the Endangered Species Act. *University Kansas Law Review, 52*, 1249–1284.

Ruhl, J. B. (2005). Regulation by Adaptive Management – Is It Possible? *Minnesota Journal of Law Science and Technology, 7*, 21–57.
Ruhl, J. B. (2008). Law's Complexity: A Primer. *Georgia State Law Review, 24*(4), 885–911.
Ruhl, J. B., & Fischman, R. (2010). Adaptive Management in the Courts. *Minnesota Law Review, 95*(2), 424–484.
Walker, B., & Salt, D. (2008). *Resilience Thinking: Sustaining Ecosystems and People in a Changing World*. London: Island Press.

Index[1]

[1] Note: Page numbers followed by 'n' refer to notes.

A. Carline et al., *Rape and the Criminal Trial*, Palgrave Socio-Legal Studies, https://doi.org/10.1007/978-3-030-38684-9

N

O

P

R

S